BUSINESS LETTERS I MADE EASY

LAWPACK

Business Letters I Made Easy
Edited by David Crosby

published by
LAWPACK

10 -16 Cole Street London SE1 4YH
www.lawpack.co.uk

Originally published as '101 Business Letters' and '101 More Business Letters' by Wyvern Publications Ltd

Text Copyright 1997 Wyvern Publications Limited
Format Copyright 1999 Law Pack Publishing Limited

ISBN 1 902646 38 X

This publication is designed to provide accurate and authoritative information in regard to subject matter covered. It is sold with the understanding that neither the publisher nor author is engaged in rendering legal, accounting, or other professional services. If legal advice or other expert assistance is required, the services of a competent professional should be sought.

Table of contents

1   Managing suppliers

2   Managing customers

3 Debt collection and credit control

Introduction to Business Letters I Made Easy™

Rattle out business letters in a fraction of the time

It is difficult to compose, write and sign a business letter in under 20 minutes. Many letters, if you think about it, can take 30 or 40 minutes, or even an hour each, just to get sorted. The morning post can be the start of a frustrating, time-consuming irritation for many managers.

It doesn't have to be that way. All the letters in this book may be copied straight from the page, and some will require only a slight amendment. With other letters, you may want to take a phrase here or a paragraph there and slot it into the rest of your letter. The important thing to remember is that the 'thinking' has already been done for you - so, those difficult situations, where you can't quite get the right words together, can now be banished ... forever.

Your time is expensive – this book could save you £££s

When a typical letter can cost a business about £15 to send out, mostly in the time of the manager composing it, anything that can bring this cost down will make a big difference. With over 100 letters in this *Made Easy* guide (each costing a fraction of this amount), it is easy to see how many pounds you can save by slicing hours off your letter writing time.

Angry letters, friendly letters, diplomatic letters, letters that get results

Identifying how subtle tones in a letter are achieved using different phrases is not always easy to pinpoint. What makes, for example, the tone in a letter of complaint either friendly, neutral, angry, diplomatic or strong? To help you find the answer, each letter in this book comes with its own incisive commentary, many of which highlight the specific words and phrases that alter the tone. The commentaries also clarify the meaning that is implicit in the words chosen, and demonstrate how a recipient will perceive and interpret those phrases, helping you to get exactly what you want.

Finding the letter you want is easy

The Guide has a comprehensive Contents page, which groups the letters by topic (Managing Suppliers, Managing Customers, etc.). Each topic is then subdivided into further categories, for example, under Managing Suppliers you will find (amongst others) Quotations, Orders, Invoices and statements, etc. Each letter is also numbered for ease of reference.

But what if you want to look up all the letters concerned with say, negotiating? All you have to do is turn to the Index of letters by type on page xiii, where a comprehensive list of these letters (and other types) will be found. For a final catch-all, there is a comprehensive topic index at the end of the work.

No matter what letter you have to write, *Business Letters I Made Easy* will repay you, not only in time saved, but also in helping you to clinch deals, get debts paid quickly, obtain better prices and persuade people to your way of thinking. Whatever the letter, I wish you every success.

More time-saving letters

Business Letters I Made Easy is a companion book to *Business Letters II Made Easy*. If you have both of them, you will have access to a wider range of business subjects and situations. Here are the topics in *Business Letters II Made Easy* not covered in this work:

- Employing staff
- Sales and marketing management
- Banking
- Insurance
- Property
- Business and the community
- International trade

While the letters in both *Business Letters I Made Easy* and *Business Letters II Made Easy* are different, we have kept the Appendices and Introduction in each volume the same. The Appendices will be one of the most sought after sections (by your colleagues as well as yourself) and we feel it is important to make this information accessible in each volume. So, if a colleague happens to 'borrow' one of the volumes, you won't be left high and dry! Unless, of course, both volumes have been 'borrowed', in which case I recommend you buy another set!

David Crosby

Acknowledgements

The Publisher would like to thank the customers who contributed letters to this guide, including: David Lambert of APTECH, Peter Le Conte of Van der Windt Packaging (UK) Ltd, DR Radia of NRG Victory Reinsurance Ltd, Eddie Mander of GCS, DRE Clark of the AEC Group of Companies Ltd and Martin Oates of BSG Products. Special thanks also to Vic Blake of Cambridge for his contributions to the work.

Index of letters by type

This index is designed to be used with the contents and the main index at the end of the book. The Contents gives a good overview of the letters concerned with suppliers, customers, employees and so on. But, if you have to write a complaining letter (and want to compare these kinds of letters), it is difficult to find them easily by examining the Contents. However, if you look up *Complaining* in this index, you will find a list of the letters featured that are concerned with this topic, by letter number.

Managing suppliers

1

Chapter 1
Managing suppliers

Suppliers often need to be held on a tight rein. Whether you need to query a quotation, place an order, negotiate a special arrangement, or simply want to make a complaint using a stern reproach, this chapter offers ideas and solutions designed to keep your suppliers firmly under your control. Just a few of the highlights are featured here.

Need to negotiate a rate with a supplier?

Suppliers may suggest a rate that is not feasible. Letter 21 shows how to clinch a deal without over-stretching your budget.

Need to negotiate a better price?

Suppliers may sometimes be tempted to nudge their prices up above the competition. If you want to keep them on their toes, try letter 4 to negotiate a keen quotation.

Need to sell a new idea to a supplier?

Sometimes you may need to change the way you want suppliers to do things for you. If a supplier has been doing it in a certain way for you for a long time you will need to sell the idea and persuade them to accept that you want it done differently. Letter 19 shows how to bring them around to your way of thinking.

Do you need to fire a strong warning shot at a supplier?

It is a common trick for a supplier to agree a competitive price but then for that price to creep up over a period. Letter 23 shows how to adopt a polite but firm stance that demonstrates to your supplier just how far you are prepared to go.

Stand up to unreasonable terms and conditions

Don't let a supplier get away with unreasonable terms and conditions. And don't fall into the trap of thinking they won't try to enforce them. Sort them out when placing your order and stand up for your rights. Remember, you are the customer. Letter 10 illustrates it in practice.

Don't shy away from changing your terms and conditions

If things are not going the way you want them to, you may have to change the terms and conditions with a supplier. Don't shy away from it just because other terms were agreed previously. Letter 20 shows how to present new terms to a supplier so that they are readily accepted and there is no quibble about them.

Making a stern reproach

When complaining, make sure that you strike the right note to produce the desired response. Too harsh, and you risk alienating your suppliers. Too soft, and they may walk all over you. Six different letters portray some of the options available to you.

The supplier here has a good existing relationship with the customer. There is no need to specify delivery instructions as the supplier knows where the parts are to be sent. The specification, though, remains clearly set out.

It is good idea to give the date by when you want the quote – this helps bring it to the top of the supplier's priorities. If he then gives you the quote after the date requested, you will be able to come down harder on him. Otherwise, you could be greeted with excuses such as 'I didn't realise it was so urgent'.

Fenner & Sons

16 George Street, Woodbridge,
Suffolk IP3 7KL
Tel: (01394) 198423
Fax: (01394) 198444
Registered in England: 91221299
VAT No: 919129075 80

Mr J M Hibberd
Sales Manager
Pecklacks (Metals) Ltd
Drovers Lane
Slough
SL42 3RG

31 May 1999

Dear Jim

I am delighted to say that our sales are ahead of expectations and so we are boosting our production. Consequently, we need more parts urgently (within ten days of placing the order). The parts are:

Item:	Part No:	Unit:	Quantity:
1.5" Aluminium Trunking	B14375	3 metre	10
Lock Nuts	J388851	each	60
2" Mild Steel Bolts	J388232	each	60
Closing Strip	B13650	3 metre	10
Steel Brackets	C18724	each	27
Steel Brackets	C18725	each	3

We shall be making our decision on Thursday 12 June, so please let me have your prices by that date.

Yours sincerely

Patrick Thompson
Production Manager

This is a standard request for a quotation. It is brief and to the point and the formality is appropriate for a new supplier. Note the specification of part numbers accompanying each item. This avoids any ambiguity about what items are to be supplied, particularly with the steel brackets, of which there are two different types.

Fenner & Sons

16 George Street, Woodbridge,
Suffolk IP3 7KL
Tel: (01394) 198423
Fax: (01394) 198444
Registered in England: 91221299
VAT No: 919129075 80

Mr J M Hibberd
Sales Manager
Pecklacks (Metals) Ltd
Drovers Lane
Slough
SL42 3RG

31 May 1999

Dear Mr Hibberd

Please supply a quotation for the following:

Item:	Part No:	Unit:	Quantity:
1.5"Aluminium Trunking	B14375	3 metre	10
Lock Nuts	J388851	each	60
2" Mild Steel Bolts	J388232	each	60
Closing Strip	B13650	3 metre	10
Steel Brackets	C18724	each	27
Steel Brackets	C18725	each	3

Delivery will be to Cardiff and we are looking for a delivery date within ten days of placing our order.

We would appreciate your quotation by fax and at the latest by Thursday 12 June.

Yours sincerely

Patrick Thompson
Production Manager

Price is often a sensitive issue between suppliers and customers. Here, a customer clearly senses that she is not being treated as well as she was by another branch of the same printing firm.

It is important not to jump to immediate conclusions and accuse the supplier of foul play. There may, after all, be a perfectly valid excuse.

The style of the two short sentences in the second paragraph ("I have just one query. The price.") puts the reader on the spot but stops short of making an accusation.

Hart & Tucker Ltd
19 Green Street, Maidstone, Kent ME41 1TJ
Telephone: (01622) 109109
Facsimile: (01622) 108106
Reg. No: England 96223978 VAT No: 91210674

Ms Sally Patterson
Sales Manager
Colourfast Printing
245 Downfields Ind. Est.
Maidstone
Kent
ME3 3ED

23 May 1999

Dear Ms Patterson

Your quotation: SL 3490
Thanks for your quotation for printing 2000 booklets.

I have just one query. The price.

As you know, I used to deal with your Halstead branch prior to our

for a related project. The extent is the same, the paper quality is the same and the quantity is the same. So why is your price 25% higher?

Yours sincerely

Jean Oilson
Production Manager

Where a customer has an existing agreement with a supplier and the supplier has chosen to forget or ignore a substantive term, a stern letter is called for. This one has the backing of the agreement which has been broken and the negotiating power that a better price can be obtained elsewhere.

The supplier has no options but to back down or face losing the business. If the customer had not obtained a more competitive quote, then the last sentence, which threatens to transfer the business, should be omitted. It wouldn't carry the same weight and a supplier may take it for what it would be – just an idle threat.

SIMPSON & MARTIN

39 TOP STREET
STOKE-ON-TRENT
ST2 3DR UNITED KINGDOM
Tel: (01782) 156232 Fax: (01782) 120899
Reg. No: England 96223978 VAT No: 91210674

Mr T Edwards
Sales Director
Bond & Bond Paper Merchants
12-16 Little Lane
Great Langdale
Ambleside
Cumbria
CU2 7BT

6 Oct 1999

Dear Tony,

Your quotation no. TE/219785
Thanks for your quotation for supplying 30 reams of 85gsm paper. I am aware the price of paper has been escalating recently but, frankly, I am not at all happy with this price or your suggestion for remedying the situation.

We had an explicit agreement that your prices would remain unchanged until the end of the calendar year. I took this to mean that all goods *ordered* before the end of the calendar year would be supplied at that year's rate. The fact that the order cannot be supplied until the new year is, frankly, not our problem.

Incidentally, I have received a quotation from a direct competitor of yours at Make-it Paper who has offered to guarantee your *original* price for the next six months.

In the light of this, may I suggest that you reconsider your quotation to us. If you are unable to match Make-it Paper's price, then I regret that we shall have no option but to transfer our business.

Yours sincerely

Mike Moy
Senior Buyer

ORDERS
Letter 5: Placing an order and requesting delivery

This is a simple letter to accompany a purchase order for a supplier with whom a credit account has not been opened.

Sending a cheque with the order should result in prompt service. Although the delivery details and date by when the goods are required should already be on the purchase order, it does no harm to spell them out in a letter as well. It also gives you the opportunity to confirm special instructions, as with the packing specifications here.

⊗ WILSON SMITH LTD

A wholly-owned subsidiary of The Wilson Group PLC
16 Willow Walk, Retford, Nottingham NG6 8WS
Tel: (01777) 121211 Fax: (01777) 121233
Reg. No: England 1212298762

Mr H Johnson
Sales Executive
P & J Electrical
Nuffield Ind. Est.
Morton, Retford
Nottingham
NG23 5TG

12 September 1999

Dear Mr. Johnson,

OUR ORDER NO. 10743
Please find our cheque to the value of £1123.60 to cover our order no. 10743. We require delivery on or by Thursday, 21st October 1999. Please ensure the items are packed in double-walled boxes, shrunk-wrapped on pallets.

Delivery address:-

Howlett & Son Ltd
Burston Industrial Estate
16 Garrard Street
Greenwich
London SE14

Please advise us of the delivery date as soon as possible.

Many thanks for your co-operation.

Yours sincerely,

Penny Taylor
Buyer

The service here is critical to the buyer. She needs the disk back urgently and is placing the order on the understanding it will be returned on a specified day. Note how she doesn't simply say she is enclosing a cheque but breaks down the charge into its various components showing how the amount is arrived at. The implication in this letter is 'if anything is different from what is specified here, I expect you to let me know'.

SIMPSON & MARTIN

39 TOP STREET
STOKE-ON-TRENT
ST2 3DR UNITED KINGDOM
Tel: (01782) 156232 Fax: (01782) 120899
Reg. No: England 96223978 VAT No: 91210674

Ms Jenny Croft
Sales Co-ordinator
CJB Services
Highfield House
Standish Industrial Estate
Wigan
WN7 9OE

23 February 1999

Dear Jenny,

Disk Conversion
Following our telephone conversation today, I enclose a copy of the Apple Mac Disk (Word 3.0) which I would like converted to Word for Windows 3.1.

I understand the charge for this is £10 + £20 for the express service + VAT. I therefore have pleasure in enclosing a cheque for £35.25.

I understand the express service means you will send the disk back the same day it is received by 1st class post. On this basis, I look forward to receiving the disk back on Friday 25 February.

As we shall be needing this service again, I would be grateful if you could arrange for an account to be opened.

Yours sincerely

Nina Rose
Publications Assistant

ORDERS
Letter 7: Amending delivery instructions

However much you plan, last-minute changes will often occur. A supplier may have already booked a carrier to deliver goods to one place and then someone else decides they should go to a different location. The opening in this letter helps to defuse any irritation that a supplier may feel, especially when he realises that the change is due to circumstances beyond your control.

Wright & Simpson

157 Colder Way
Basingstoke
Hants RG21 5TG
Tel: (01256) 125907
Fax: (01256) 190986

Mr J Matthews
Sales Manager
Bull (Prints) Limited
Tillman's Trading Estate
Bristol
BS21 2LG

23 June 1999

Dear Julian

Re: Our Order No. 11978
I am sorry if this messes you around but our client has just notified us that they would like their order delivered into a different warehouse. The goods should now be sent to:

Hobbles (Cambridge) Limited
Eagle Trading Estate
Colchester Road
Basildon
Essex
B4 9UO

I hope this doesn't cause you too much inconvenience.

Many thanks for your co-operation.

Yours sincerely

Edward Wright

Partners: EG Wright MA & FA Simpson

ORDERS
Letter 8: Amending the order quantity

If you do make a mistake, it is best to sort it out as soon as possible. This letter would be written to a supplier who is well known to you.

The unconventional opening contains an element of surprise, signifying that it is not just a piece of routine correspondence, but something that demands immediate attention. The friendly tone also sets the scene for the supplier to forgive you for overlooking something so simple and, importantly, tells them immediately that it is not his fault.

 # WILSON SMITH LTD

A wholly-owned subsidiary of The Wilson Group PLC
16 Willow Walk, Retford, Nottingham NG6 8WS
Tel: (01777) 121211 Fax: (01777) 121233
Reg. No: England 1212298762

Facsimile Message

To:	RPP Holdings plc
F.A.O.:	Bob Taylor
From:	Tom Greate
Date:	23 August 1999
No. of Pages:	1

Dear Bob

Wilson Smith Quality Manual
Oops! We've made a real clanger.

Don has just created a sample of the contents for our quality manual, which he has inserted into the ringbinder – only to discover that the binder is too small. It seems that someone here interpreted the extent of 350 *leaves* as 350 *pages*.

Is it too late to change the order? I tried to call you but your phone was continuously engaged, so I am faxing this to you instead.

Please call me back urgently so we can discuss this.

Yours sincerely

Tom Greate
Quality Manager

ORDERS
Letter 9: Ticking off a supplier for not sticking to the order

The tone of this curt letter is designed to bring the supplier sharply into line. You need to be a little careful to ensure you are not over-reacting to the situation. It would be appropriate for a supplier who had ignored similar requests in the past.

The last comment "I look forward to continuing our business relationship on a more organised note" is in danger of putting the reader's back up as it sounds like a personal attack – even if it is not intended that way. It could be rephrased as 'I trust our purchase order instructions will be rigidly adhered to in future', which apportions no blame but gets the same message across.

 RPP Holdings Plc
35/38 New Road, Paignton, Devon TQ3 4UU
Tel: 01803 175653 Fax: 01803 187908
Reg. No: England 1976143

Mr J Patel
Sales Co-ordinator
Charles Bright Limited
63 Crow Lane
Brentwood
Essex
CM15 2AM

28 September 1999

Dear Mr Patel,

Our purchase order no. R467985
Thank you for your latest delivery, received today.

I would like to draw to your attention a very important point, which has been missed with the processing of this order.

On the purchase order, it is stated that your delivery note must be marked for the attention of Thomas Jones and, more importantly, contain our purchase order number. This is vital to us when we are receiving hundreds of items a day.

As this is a new request from us, we shall not be delaying payment as stated on the order but please bear this arrangement in mind for future business.

I hope you will appreciate the necessity behind this instruction and I look forward to continuing our business relationship on a more organised note.

Yours sincerely

Nina Lynch
Purchasing Manager

When you start trading with a new company, it is important to check on and agree the terms and conditions of supply. It is no use the supplier sending his quotation, listing his terms and conditions of supply, and then you sending your purchase order with its terms and conditions of purchase, and hoping that will do. What happens later on if there is a dispute? It is far better to clarify at the outset conflicting terms.

One of the commonest areas that is open to misinterpretation is what is meant by 30 days' credit. Is it literally 30 days from the date of the invoice? Or is the interpretation that the buying company makes here correct? Make sure you are clear about what is meant.

There are two phrases to note here: "...subject to...", which is very useful when you want to qualify a particular term and "...we reserve the right to...", which is handy when you want the option, but not the obligation, to do something.

IDENDEN INDUSTRIES
A division of Idenden Plc
Porter House, Hull HU7 4RF England

Tel 01482 119087 Fax 01482 119088
Registered in England No: 1218943

Mr G Glover
Sales Manager
Christian Engineering
Rochdale Road
Middleton
Manchester
M24 5TH

14 July 1999

Dear Gordon,

PURCHASE ORDER NO. 298745
Here is our purchase order no. 298745 for the boxes. Please let your accounts people know that they must quote this purchase order number on all invoices and correspondence, otherwise payment will be delayed.

Please also note the following points regarding the terms and conditions:

Clause 4 Terms
Your payment terms of 30 days are subject to the timing of our payment runs. We settle all invoices at the end of the month in which they fall due for payment. An invoice dated 25th August, for example, will be paid on 30th September, as will an invoice dated 5th August. Accordingly, we cannot accept your interest on overdue accounts as some may appear to be overdue when they are not.

Clause 13 Quantity
We are not prepared to pay a premium to ensure delivery of the exact order quantity so we must accept that there may be some slight variation. However, we reserve the right to return over deliveries rather than pay for them, if they are not needed.

Clause 19 Intellectual Property
I do not accept this clause as written. Any copyright you own, you will continue to own. Any copyright we own, we will continue to own. Your work on our behalf does not entitle you to copyright on anything we have designed.

Clause 21 Title & Risk in the goods.
We do not accept clause (b). It is your responsibility to ensure safe delivery of the goods to us. We will not become liable to pay for any goods that do not reach us in satisfactory condition.

Finally, I enclose the customer credit application form duly completed and signed. It is subject to the contents of this letter.

Yours sincerely

Michael Preston
Marketing Manager

Someone has processed an order incorrectly and the wrong goods have been sent. A common enough mistake. This letter explains to the person in accounts exactly what the position is and why payment is not being made against the invoice. It ends on a reassuring note, saying to them when payment for other outstanding items will be made.

B & R HENDERSONS LTD
Marlows Road, Aberdeen AB20 5GT
Tel: 01224 267855 Fax: 01224 267977
Reg. No: 16497811 VAT No: 7387945

Frank O'Neil
Marketing Manager
Benton Copleys
Roundtree House
Kennet
Newmarket
CB8 7LP

25 April 1999

Dear Frank,

Your invoice no. 143880
I have received your statement requesting payment of invoice no. 143880 for £156.77, dated 30 July.

I understand that the items received against this invoice were sent in error and the goods ordered are out of stock at your warehouse.

Please could you arrange for a credit note to be issued for the full amount of £156.77. We shall be settling the remaining invoices at the end of this month.

Yours sincerely

David Barker
Purchasing Manager

Occasionally the wrong goods may be sent to the wrong company – or someone has circumvented normal procedures when buying them. Although the goods probably aren't intended for your company, it is best to check first with the supplier, just in case. Asking for the supplier's reference should help get to the bottom of the story. It would be more embarrassing to return the goods, only to find that someone high up had placed the order but not told anyone! Discretion is the better part of valour.

⊛ WILSON SMITH LTD

A wholly-owned subsidiary of The Wilson Group PLC
16 Willow Walk, Retford, Nottingham NG6 8WS
Tel: (01777) 121211 Fax: (01777) 121233
Reg. No: England 1212298762

Mr Trevor Goodge
Sales Manager
Idenden Industries
Porter House
Hull
HU7 4RF

15 June 1999

Dear Trevor,

Your invoice no. 85903

I have received in the post this morning your invoice no. 85903 for £300.80 for 40 high pressure seal rings.

We have no record of placing this order and your invoice omits to provide a reference. All our orders must be made on a valid purchase order and signed by an authorised signatory. I have checked with my colleagues to see if anyone has ordered these items and accidentally omitted to draft a purchase order but no one recalls placing such an order.

Before we return the goods to you, please could you let me know what reference you have for this order and I will look into the matter further for you.

Yours sincerely

Jim Bone
Purchasing Manager

INVOICES AND STATEMENTS
Letter 13: Disputing a carriage charge

Carriage charges are often a source of contention. Companies supplying goods are aware that it costs a lot of money to deliver them. Equally, the business placing the order wants to keep the price as low as possible.

Some invoices may carry a carriage charge, added automatically when they are produced. This could explain how this 'error' occurred – or it could be a case of the supplier trying it on. Either way, a short letter, backed up with the knowledge that you had specified carriage be included in the quote, should put matters straight. "I was surprised ..." sets a gentle but firm tone for the reader.

Thomas King
& Palmer Ltd
serving the world

24 Fuller Road, Welling,
Kent DA16 7JP
Tel : (01322) 100132
Fax : (01322) 100178

Reg. No : England 1212298762
VAT No : 92905643

Henry Fuller
Sales Manager
Savill Plastics Ltd
Saxon Way
Hitchin
Herts
HN7 5TG

23 June 1999

Dear Henry,

Your invoice no. 29783
Thank you for your invoice no. 29783 for £7800.

I was surprised to see a carriage charge included for £69. Your original quotation (no. LM89753) made no mention of an additional charge for delivery. As our purchase order specified that the goods be delivered carriage paid I was led to believe that this was included in your quotation.

Please could you send us a credit note for the full amount of the carriage.

Yours sincerely

Alan Scott
Purchasing Manager

Note the tone used to handle the unexpected charge here. The letter offers no thanks to the company for sending the invoice but uses the more neutral "I have received..." This forewarns the reader that all may not be well.

The second paragraph has a more demonstrative tone, with useful emphatic expressions such as: "No mention was made..." and the firm "...referred expressly to the fact...". Remember, if you use the term 'expressly' the point must have been definitely stated (preferably in writing) and not implied.

Charles Cunningham Ltd

29 Baker Street, LONDON N34 6GH England
Tel: (0171) 015 1290 Fax: (0171) 015 1271
Reg. No: England 1104398135 VAT No: 82108643

Adams Office Supplies
Brentwood Road
Fulham
London
SW6 8JM

22 March 1999

Dear Sir / Madam

Your invoice number DL67501

I have received your invoice for the departmental shredder which was ordered.   I note that the invoice amount includes a delivery charge of £25.50.

When we placed our order, no mention was made by your sales representative of this charge and our Purchase Order No. WR15498 referred expressly to the fact that delivery was to be included within the price quoted. This was not queried prior to receipt of the shredder.

I look forward to receiving a credit note for the full amount of £25.50.

Yours faithfully

Joan Smith
Office Manager

Product catalogues are not always clear and often omit information that a customer wants. In this letter, the potential customer has four pieces of information that he needs to know before making a decision to buy.

When faced with a number of questions, setting them out as a numbered list helps the reader to assimilate quickly what information is being asked for. The writer could just as easily have presented the items as bullet points, but it is easier for a respondent to refer to a number in a reply (especially in long lists) than to have to explain which point is being talked about.

Grange & Turner Ltd

32 WESTBOURN ROAD, WITNEY, OXON OX6 7HY

Telephone (01993) 107888
Fax (01993) 107843

Reg. No: England 13078453
VAT No: 75698764

Mr E Thomas
Sales Administator
Starbright Office Supplies
Wilmslow Road
Didcot
Oxon
OX7 5GH

20 March 1999

Dear Mr Thomas

Fax machines
I have received your catalogue of fax machines. Before I decide which model to purchase, please could you advise me about the facilities for the Sharp UX3500 and Panasonic UF321 machines:

1. What is the automatic feed capacity of each machine?

2. Will both machines accept A3 size paper?

3. What is the print resolution of the Sharp model?

4. When the catalogue refers to transmission speed in seconds, is this the speed it takes for one A4 sheet of paper to be transmitted?

Yours sincerely

John Sand
Office Manager

Not everything can be bought off the shelf by simply quoting a product name and price. With professional services, there will be a process of exploring what is required before agreeing terms. This letter seeks a consultant to help implement the ISO 9000 standard.

The writer could have given more details about the size of the company – how many employees there are, size of turnover, breakdown of the activities and so on. But equally, these will occur in the course of the subsequent telephone conversation. It may even be preferable to arouse the reader's curiosity – a useful tactic to ensure a swift response.

It is always useful to say how you got hold of their name. If it was a referral and you are competing for attention, naming your common source can help to build a rapport. Note the close. Thanking the recipient before he has even responded is a convenient way of putting an obligation on him to reply.

Grange & Turner Ltd

32 WESTBOURN ROAD, WITNEY, OXON OX6 7HY

Telephone (01993) 107888
Fax (01993) 107843

Reg. No: England 13078453
VAT No: 75698764

Mr Tom Patterson
Managing Partner
T P Consultancy
234 Slade Street
Milton Keynes
MK43 7PL

7 August 1999

Dear Mr Patterson,

We are a small company specialising in business-to-business direct marketing. We are coming under increasing pressure from our clients to implement the BS EN ISO 9000 specification. We would therefore be interested to find out exactly what this would involve, in terms of man hours, cost and procedures.

Your name was passed to me by the Association of Quality Management Consultants as someone who is registered to advise in this area. I would be most grateful if you would agree to visit us and give us an introduction to the requirements, which I understand would be free of charge.

If you are available, please would you ring me at the above number to fix a mutually convenient time.

Thank you for your kind attention. I look forward to hearing from you.

Yours sincerely

William Barker
Marketing Director

REQUESTS, ENQUIRIES AND INSTRUCTIONS
Letter 17: Advising existing suppliers of a change in terms and conditions

Terms and conditions of supply should regularly be reviewed by companies. Sometimes they will need to be amended; if they do, a letter like this will be sufficient. Don't forget to include the date from when the new terms apply.

If the change is more significant than the one shown here – for example, changing payment terms to 60 days' from 30 days' – you should get written confirmation from the supplier that he agrees to the change, to avoid subsequent disputes. This could be done by asking him to countersign an enclosed copy of the letter and return it to you.

GKT Products Ltd, Unit 10, Castleway Lane, Alloway, Ayr, KA7 4BE
Telephone (01292) 177900 Fax (01292) 199855 Reg. No: 17964583 VAT No: 679845

The Sales Manager
SLP Engineering
27 Vine Street
Penrith
Cumbria
CA9 3FV

3 June 1999

Dear Sir / Madam

Amendment to terms and conditions
I am writing to advise you of a change in our terms and conditions, which affects all orders placed with us from 1 July.

All delivery notes accompanying goods supplied to us must contain the correct purchase order number. This will enable us to match up the relevant paperwork more quickly and prevent any delays in payment to you.

Thank you for your cooperation in this matter.

Yours faithfully

Jean Hardcastle
Accounts Manager

REQUESTS, ENQUIRIES AND INSTRUCTIONS
Letter 18: Advising a supplier of delivery instructions

Delivery instructions often need to be given after an order has been placed. If more than one order from your company is going through the supplier at any one time, you need to make sure the original purchase order number is given, to avoid confusion.

Delivery instructions should also give a contact name and be marked for the attention of a named person. It can be all too easy for goods to be delivered to a company and for the person who placed the order to be the last to find out, because none of the accompanying documentation gives his or her name.

 **RPP**

RPP Holdings Plc
35/38 New Road, Paignton, Devon TQ3 4UU
Tel: 01803 175653 Fax: 01803 187908
Reg. No: England 1976143

Jane Summers
Marketing Executive
Corrugated Card & Packaging Ltd
Unit 8 London Road Ind. Est.
Truro
Cornwall
TR9 7KM

27 July 1999

Dear Jane,

Purchase order number 548792
Please arrange for the consignment of 500 cardboard boxes to be delivered to our Middleton warehouse. The address is:

Unit 4
The Middleton Business Park
Angles Lane
Middleton
MD3 4XZ

The consignment should be marked for the attention of Mr Jeff Holmes, our Warehouse Manager.

Yours sincerely

Helen Meeting
Supplies Manager

A supplier is questioning a new procedure that has been forced upon him. Here the supplier's customer is persuading the supplier to accept the change of policy. Note how it is being 'sold' to the supplier, not as something new but as something which he should have been doing anyway: "...it should be little more than an extension of what your current practices are...". This is a neat argument, against which there is little defence.

B & R HENDERSONS LTD
Marlows Road, Aberdeen AB20 5GT
Tel: 01224 267855 Fax: 01224 267977
Reg. No: 16497811 VAT No: 7387945

Robert Noyes
Sales Manager
NPB Manufacturing Ltd
4 Manor Close
Warrington
WA3 3HY

20 August 1999

Dear Robert,

Re: Progress Sheets
Thank you for your recent faxes, and I apologise for the delay in replying.

First of all, I would like to reassure you that our policy of demanding progress sheets, properly signed and dated, is designed to protect both you and other suppliers involved in the manufacturing process. With this system in place, if a problem arises at any stage in the process we will have a better idea of where the fault might lie. It also aims to catch any hitches at the start of the process, rather than on the day that our goods are meant to be delivered. All we are doing is formalising the procedure that we have always asked our subcontractors and printers to follow (see our letter 24.06.99) but that, in practice, has not been carried out.

It is not intended to be a sword hanging over anyone's head – it should be little more than an extension of what your current practices are. All our suppliers have been asked to comply with this new policy, since everyone has experienced problems in the past.

I hope this explains our reason for implementing the system satisfactorily and trust that you will be able to co-operate with its operation. Should you be uncertain about any aspect of it, please do not hesitate to give us a call.

Yours sincerely

Roger McIntyre
Manager

NEGOTIATING ARRANGEMENTS
Letter 20: Informing a supplier of changed terms and conditions

You may at some time need to revise your systems if you find that they are not working well. Note how the suggestion here starts off relatively softly "...this is what we propose..." and "...we would be very grateful for your co-operation...", aiming to win the supplier over.

However, the implementation of a 'stick' element in "...we will be adding a penalty clause..." noticeably gives the supplier no choice, even though the first part sounds as if the supplier has a say in the matter. This is confirmed by the closing line, which doesn't ask for their reaction but simply presents it as a *fait accompli*.

Grange & Turner Ltd

32 WESTBOURN ROAD, WITNEY, OXON OX6 7HY

Telephone (01993) 107888
Fax (01993) 107843

Reg. No: England 13078453
VAT No: 75698764

Terry Coles
Sales Manager
C & D Print Services
33 Top Street
Aldermaston
Reading
RG7 8JU

22 November 1999

Dear Terry

Re: Deliveries

As you know

Over the last year or so <u>all</u> have had at least one problem, due to insufficiently labelled deliveries.

We have tried to suggest systems to help both printer and supplier to prevent this problem, but on the whole, we have been politely ignored (or conveniently forgotten), once the immediate problem is over.

So we now feel that we have to insist that a good system for recording deliveries is

All boxes of printed matter should in future be labelled as follows:

1. Sample of the contents on top of the box
2. On the side of the box:
   - Quantity of items in the box
   - Scratch code of the item
   - Promotion code

   There should be no other codes, which may cause confusion on the boxes.
3. On the dispatch note: total quantity of each item, by scratch code.

Our suppliers to whom you send items will be required to count in the boxes and confirm that the quantity supplied matches the dispatch note, and that there are sufficient boxes as indicated by the Job Sheet supplied by us. They will also be required to fax us a confirmation of the quantity received and any shortfall. This will also ensure that any problems are noted in good time, to prevent delivery being delayed.

We would be very grateful for your co-operation in this, which is designed to protect all of us. To assist with its compliance, we will be adding a penalty clause, with immediate effect, that a failure to label the boxes and count them in to the mailing house correctly will result in delay of payment of 30 days <u>beyond</u> our normal credit terms with you.

Thank you for your assistance in this matter.

Yours sincerely

Helen Mace
Production Manager

NEGOTIATING ARRANGEMENTS
Letter 21: Negotiating a rate with a supplier

If a supplier suggests a rate for a job that is not feasible it may be better to go back to them with a fixed figure that you are prepared to spend and see if an agreement can be reached.

The friendly tone will reassure the supplier that the intention is sincere and it is not simply a question of trying to tie him down on price. The rhetorical question at the end "Are you game?" acts as a challenge and is designed to clinch the deal.

Thomas King & Palmer Ltd
serving the world

24 Fuller Road, Welling,
Kent DA16 7JP
Tel : (01322) 100132
Fax : (01322) 100178

Reg. No : England 1212298762
VAT No : 92905643

Mr D R West
67 Millers Lane
Tackley
Oxford
OX6 3AG

26 May 1999

Dear David,

Corporate newsletter

Thanks for your fax of 9th May. Sorry that I have sat on it for so long – particularly as my need is so urgent!!

While a daily charge sounds logical, I am uncomfortable with it because neither of us knows how long these things are going to take to produce. And anyway, some will take longer than others, depending on the available resources.

So, I have an alternative suggestion to make which, I think, is fair.

We put £350 *per newsletter* on the table to write it. So, following a thorough discussion and briefing, you do what you feel is reasonable for that amount of money. The intention is not to squeeze a quart out of a pint pot. It is to see what we can achieve within that sort of budget. Are you game?

I look forward to hearing from you.

Kind regards

Yours sincerely

Kay Mitchell
Marketing Manager

Declining a supplier politely is not always easy. This letter strikes an agreeable but firm tone. The politeness of the decline is helped by going for the understatement: "...it does not fit comfortably..." which contrasts with the firmer "Thanks but no thanks", which is refreshingly frank and leaves no doubt about the decision, so nobody's time is wasted.

What goes unsaid is often as important as what is said. Note how the customer does not offer any hope for the future – a clear sign that the products the supplier produces are unsuitable for this market.

Grange & Turner Ltd

32 WESTBOURN ROAD, WITNEY, OXON OX6 7HY

Telephone (01993) 107888
Fax (01993) 107843

Reg. No: England 13078453
VAT No: 75698764

Mr A French
Sales Administator
Squeeky Kleen
45 Todd Square
Glasgow
G20 5XA

28 September 1999

Dear Mr French

<u>Squeeky-kleen</u>
Thank you for your letter of 11th September and for the samples of your innovative cleaning product.

At the moment, it does not fit comfortably with our catalogue plans for the next six months and I am afraid I must say "Thanks but no thanks".

If you are thinking of doing any direct mail of your own on the product, we do have a strong mailing list of corporate customers who have bought related items. If you are interested in renting these, do give me a call.

Yours sincerely

Brian Reed
Marketing Manager

NEGOTIATING ARRANGEMENTS
Letter 23: Firing a strong warning shot at a supplier

This letter is designed to send a strong message. It tries to make the supplier face up to the reality of the situation.

It starts off gently but firmly: "The unfortunate fact of the matter...". Note how the additional expense is very slightly exaggerated (or made to appear more serious) by adding the words "...up to £400...", £400 being the worst case, not the average case.

A polite but firm stance is maintained to the end "...we will probably have to agree to part company...", the 'probably' leaving the door open for further negotiations but signalling at the same time how far you are prepared to go.

Hart & Tucker Ltd
19 Green Street, Maidstone, Kent ME41 1TJ
Telephone: (01622) 109109
Facsimile: (01622) 108106
Reg. No: England 96223978 VAT No: 91210674

Terry Coles
Sales Manager
C & D Print Services
33 Top Street
Aldermaston
Reading
RG7 8JU

22 September 1999

Dear Terry

Re: Your charges
Thank you for your letter of 12th September and for taking the trouble to clarify the situation for me. I am sorry that I had to ask you to do this because our files had got into such a mess.

I can see that I must accept the invoices raised on promotions 102 and 109 as having been agreed. However, I believe that Claire is still waiting for a breakdown of your invoice for order 118. We are not satisfied that there was £300 of origination work required when we sent you all new film and we are also disputing the charge for the amendments.

Next year
The unfortunate fact of the matter is that with these carriage and origination charges, as well as the higher base price of £1100, it has cost us up to £400 a month *more* to put work through you rather than through our other printers. And we have no control over the variables - we don't know whether carriage is going to be £200 or £500 for the year. We don't know whether the proofs are going to be £90 or £500 a time.

There is no question about the quality of your work. It is comparable with the quality we receive from our other suppliers. But the price you charge for our jobs is simply too high.

I am afraid that, unless you can find a way to do our printing profitably for a flat rate of £1100, we will probably have to agree to part company.

Yours sincerely

Tony Green
Marketing Director

When the wrong goods are sent, you want the error to be corrected quickly. Here someone has inverted the numbers 60 and 30 for the quantity and size. A simple request to have them changed should be sufficient. The invoice will have mentioned the correct quantity and size, so this doesn't need to be changed. It should, however, be referred to in the letter, so the company can identify it on its system easily. Note how the writer tries to avoid the confusion by putting the quantity (sixty) in words and the size (30) in numbers.

If you do return goods to a company, always send them separately from a letter asking for replacements. Returns often get put to one side to be dealt with later – sometimes weeks later. It could be disastrous if your letter requesting corrective action is held up amongst the returns.

IDENDEN INDUSTRIES
A division of Idenden Plc
Porter House, Hull HU7 4RF England

Tel 01482 119087 Fax 01482 119088
Registered in England No: 1218943

Ms Elizabeth Taylor
Sales Co-ordinator
Litson & Fulton Ltd
Unit 8 Clifton Ind. Est.
Clifton Road
Liverpool
L9 6DD

24 October 1999

Dear Elizabeth,

Our purchase order no. YTL8906
Yesterday, we received sixty 30mm clips for high velocity piping, which were supplied against your invoice no LP1018 dated 20 October.

Our purchase order no. YTL8906 clearly asked for thirty 60 mm clips. I would be grateful if you could supply the correct items to us by return.

The 30mm clips are being returned to you under separate cover.

Yours sincerely

Stuart O'Neil
Purchasing Manager

ERRORS
Letter 25: Returning an incorrect consignment

Which style should be used in letters: 'I' or 'we'?

If you are writing on behalf of your company and you want the letter to sound as if it has the full weight of your organisation behind you, opt for 'we' and 'our'. If you are writing in your own right then 'I' and 'my' is preferable.

In practice there is very little to choose between the two styles although 'we' and 'our' can, in some situations, sound a touch formal. It may also be that the person writing doesn't want to take personal responsibility for what is being said in the letter.

IDENDEN INDUSTRIES
A division of Idenden Plc
Porter House, Hull HU7 4RF England

Tel 01482 119087 Fax 01482 119088
Registered in England No: 1218943

Ms Elizabeth Taylor
Sales Co-ordinator
Litson & Fulton Ltd
Unit 8 Clifton Ind. Est
Clifton Road
Liverpool
L9 6DD

24 October 1999

Dear Elizabeth,

Our order no. YTL9901
Today, your carrier attempted to deliver thirty 60mm clips for high velocity piping, in response to our order no. YTL9901.

We examined the clips and found they do not correspond with samples we received from you on 18th October, and we therefore refused to accept them.

The carrier was instructed to return them to you. We look forward to receiving correct, replacement goods as soon as possible, and your confirmation of this.

Yours sincerely

Stuart O'Neil
Purchasing Manager

MAKING COMPLAINTS – FRIENDLY AND FIRM APPROACHES
Letter 26: Gentle complaint to a good supplier – keeping him on his toes

This letter aims to present a complaint under the guise of good humour. Its tone opts for a mid-way between the formal and very casual. It succeeds in building a rapport with the reader, which will make him want to come back and put the window right.

Helen Meeting is unconcerned exactly when it will be done because she knows she can rely on John Fuller to fix the problem. The letter suggests a trust between the two which more formal business letters don't imply.

RPP Holdings Plc
35/38 New Road, Paignton, Devon TQ3 4UU
Tel: 01803 175653 Fax: 01803 187908
Reg. No: England 1976143

John Fuller
Works Manager
RG Fuller & Sons
53 Jackson Way
Tiverton
Devon
TV7 4HG

1 October 1999

Dear John

Thanks for coming to put the additional window in our office. It has really helped to lighten up the room. However, there is one minor point I want to raise with you.

For some reason, the part of the window that opens doesn't seem to want to stay in its correct position and has shuffled itself along, so that one side is scraping against the frame while the other side has an unusually large gap. Fine for a bit of ventilation in the summer months but not so pleasant when we have a howling gale!

Could you call round some time next week to have a look at it and encourage it back to its proper position? Give me a call to let me know when you are coming.

Yours sincerely

Helen Meeting
Office Manager

MAKING COMPLAINTS – FRIENDLY AND FIRM APPROACHES
Letter 27: Friendly complaint about repeated missing items

This fairly unconventional letter should be reserved for people with whom you have built up a good relationship and have a clear understanding.

A jokey response like this (particularly when it is in a complaint setting) should score you many points with your supplier. Its aim is to evoke a positive reaction in the reader so that they feel more inclined to respond favourably to your request. Its danger, which you should be aware of, is that your supplier takes you for granted and thinks that, because you are taking a light-hearted approach, you are prepared to put up with the poor service.

Note how a more casual tone is created by using abbreviated phrases and terms: "Thanks for" instead of the more formal "Thank you for" and "ASAP" in place of "as soon as possible".

RPP Holdings Plc
35/38 New Road, Paignton, Devon TQ3 4UU
Tel: 01803 175653 Fax: 01803 187908
Reg. No: England 1976143

Jane Summers
Marketing Executive
Corrugated Card & Packaging Ltd
Unit 8
London Road Ind. Est.
Truro
Cornwall
TR9 7KM

1 October 1999

Dear Jane

Purchase order number 548792

Thanks for your delivery of cardboard boxes received yesterday.

Once again, gremlins appear to have intervened and kidnapped 49 cardboard boxes out of the consignment. We are waiting for the ransom demand. Or perhaps they were hijacked by homeless people looking for a new cardboard duvet for the night?

Please, please, please supply us with the missing items ASAP.

Yours sincerely

Helen Meeting
Office Manager

MAKING COMPLAINTS – FRIENDLY AND FIRM APPROACHES
Letter 28: Complaining about repeatedly missing items

When mistakes are repeatedly being made, customers are justified in raising their hackles. The tone of the letter is one of irritation. But it doesn't seek to blame. Instead it points out the need to improve matters because everyone is suffering. Ranting and railing on its own is often pointless – it may feel good but it is usually better to suggest a constructive solution, or at least, as here, to sit down and talk about the issues.

RPP Holdings Plc
35/38 New Road, Paignton, Devon TQ3 4UU
Tel: 01803 175653 Fax: 01803 187908
Reg. No: England 1976143

Jane Summers
Marketing Executive
Corrugated Card & Packaging Ltd
Unit 8
London Road Ind. Est.
Truro
Cornwall
TR9 7KM

12 December 1999

Dear Jane

Purchase order number 548792
We received your delivery of 500 cardboard boxes yesterday.

When our Warehouse Manager checked the number of boxes that had been supplied, he discovered that 49 were missing. As you know this is the fifth time in a row that there has been a shortfall in the delivery. This causes us inconvenience, you extra expense and both of us aggravation. Could I suggest that you set up a meeting between us and your Warehouse Manager, to discuss what can be done to improve matters? If deliveries do not then improve, I regret we shall have to consider turning to a more reliable supplier.

In the meantime, please arrange for the balance to be supplied as soon as possible.

Yours sincerely

Helen Meeting
Office Manager

The aim of this letter is to fire a warning shot at the supplier and shake him into changing his attitude towards you.

Clearly, the supplier has taken your company's business for granted for too long. The poor performance is made to sound worse when contrasted against the "impeccable" service that you received at the outset. The catalogue of general mistakes is then supported by a specific incident that has finally broken your faith in the supplier.

If the supplier has the will, he will make the changes, but if he doesn't make amends then the customer leaves no doubt that the business will go elsewhere: "We shall have no option ..." emphasises how far you are prepared to go. It is a useful phrase that is very handy in negotiations. Beware of using it lightly though: if you say it, make sure you are prepared to carry it out.

B & R HENDERSONS LTD

Marlows Road, Aberdeen AB20 5GT
Tel: 01224 267855 Fax: 01224 267977
Reg. No: 16497811 VAT No: 7387945

Mr Andrew McBride
Manager
Scottish Stationery Supplies
45 High Road
Aberdeen
AB19 2EW

26 July 1999

Dear Andrew,

I am writing to express my growing dissatisfaction with the service we are receiving from Scottish Stationery Supplies.

For the first year, the service you gave us was impeccable. Since then, though, we have noticed a gradual deterioration. The goods are frequently out of stock or taking longer for you to supply; you do not respond to our requests as speedily as before and the number of incorrect items delivered has increased. This was compounded this morning when, for the second time in a row, you supplied us with 5 boxes of C5 instead of C6 envelopes.

It is essential that all our suppliers give us the best possible service. We shall be monitoring the situation closely over the coming weeks, but if a significant improvement is not noticeable we shall have no option but to seek an alternative supplier.

Yours sincerely

Tina Vail
Office Manager

MAKING COMPLAINTS – FRIENDLY AND FIRM APPROACHES
Letter 30: Demanding that defective work be made good

When asking for repairs to be done, you need to emphasise how serious the situation is. Here, the work seemed satisfactory when it was done but within a short period it is clear that all is not well.

This letter leaves the request to put it right until the end. Blame is not apportioned directly (it could be the fault of the type of cement used) but note the use of the phrase "...come and remedy the defective work...", which implies heavily that the supplier is being held responsible.

SIMPSON
& MARTIN

39 TOP STREET
STOKE-ON-TRENT
ST2 3DR UNITED KINGDOM
Tel: (01782) 156232 Fax: (01782) 120899
Reg. No: England 96223978 VAT No: 91210674

Mr R Henderson
JKB Builders
16 Ponts Hill
Wysall
Stoke-on-Trent
ST4 5HT

23 September 1999

Dear Mr Henderson,

39 Top Street, Stoke-on-Trent
A week ago you arranged for a 3-foot high boundary wall to be repaired outside our property.

The work was completed to our specification, but this morning it was noticed that the mortar used to bind the bricks together has cracked, to such an extent that it is not only flaking away but several of the bricks are now in danger of becoming loose.

Would you kindly arrange for someone to come and remedy the defective work as soon as possible?

Yours sincerely

John Good
Managing Director

MAKING COMPLAINTS – FRIENDLY AND FIRM APPROACHES
Letter 31: Non-delivery of goods – initial letter

The delays that have occurred here are not serious and the customer did not make it a condition of the contract that time should be of the essence. To start issuing threats of taking your business elsewhere, therefore, would not fit the circumstances. Nevertheless, the customer is being inconvenienced. A plea for the supplier to give it "your most urgent attention" should be sufficient to get the wheels moving.

Taylor Taylor & Shaw
Benton House, Clifton, Bristol BS16 7LJ
Tel: (0117) 1089254   Fax: (0117) 1089211

Mr N Stacey
N Stacey & Co Ltd
Amber House
Grant Mill
Bristol
BS6 4RE

16 September 1999

Dear Mr Stacey,

Our purchase order no. AB46972 dated 6 September
On the 6th September, we placed an order with your company for a portable air conditioner (model no A132487). Our purchase order no. is AB46972.

When the order was placed, I was informed that you were temporarily out of stock of this item but that you had more on order and we could expect delivery within one week.

When I contacted your office on the 13th September, I was told that the air conditioner would arrive the next day. Three days have now passed and there is still no sign of a delivery or an explanation from yourselves.

Please give this matter your most urgent attention.

Yours sincerely,

AW Taylor

Partners: AW Taylor & GS Taylor

The delay has now become unacceptable and it is fully justifiable to threaten to cancel the order.

When writing letters like this, it is a good ploy to make use of certain emotional triggers, such as "You will understand that, as a business, we put a high premium on reliability". This is designed to provoke the response 'but so do we'. If it has the right effect, the supplier will pull out all the stops to deliver the item on time or, at the very least, to tell the customer what the situation is immediately.

Taylor Taylor & Shaw

Benton House, Clifton, Bristol BS16 7LJ
Tel: (0117) 1089254   Fax: (0117) 1089211

Mr N Stacey
N Stacey & Co Ltd
Amber House
Grant Mill
Bristol
BS6 4RE

28 September 1999

Dear Mr Stacey,

Re: Our order no. AB46972, dated 6 September

I wrote to you on the 16th September, chasing the above order for a portable air conditioner model no. A132487.

In spite of my letter and several phone calls, this order is still outstanding and is now very urgently required.

When placing the order on the 6th September, we were told there would be a delay of only four days. Four weeks have now passed without an explanation from yourselves. Please telephone me on receipt of this letter with a new and definite date for delivery.

You will understand that, as a business, we put a high premium on reliability. If I do not receive your call, or if further delays are expected, this order will be cancelled and our business will be taken elsewhere.

Yours sincerely

AW Taylor

Partners: AW Taylor & GS Taylor

MAKING COMPLAINTS – USING A STRONGER TONE
Letter 33: Getting a too-persistent sales representative off your back

This letter is strongly worded but wisely stops short of using anger to make its impact felt.

Showing that you have already considered several times whether to complain, adds weight to your justification in complaining now. It tells the reader that you are not over-reacting but that your patience has been tested.

The overall message is clear: the salesman's behaviour is reflecting badly on his company, and has reached such a state that you want nothing whatever to do with it.

If the writer had been tempted to show his anger, it would have undermined his credibility and inclined the reader to take the matter less seriously.

IDENDEN INDUSTRIES
A division of Idenden Plc
Porter House, Hull HU7 4RF England

Tel 01482 119087 Fax 01482 119088
Registered in England No: 1218943

Mr L Hines
Managing Director
Banks & Banister Ltd
The Old Exchange
Cambridge Road
Brampton
Cumbria
CA4 7MK

17 April 1999

Dear Mr Hines

John Higgins
I had hoped that I would not have to write to you about the activities of your company representative John Higgins, but his behaviour finally leaves me no option.

He has persistently called our office in an attempt to sell us one of your photocopiers. He has been told repeatedly that we have no requirements for any photocopiers and that we are very happy with our existing supplier. Today, he called my secretary and claimed that he was a close friend so that he would be put through. I regard this behaviour as totally unprofessional. His only success to date has been to increase my resolve that we shall never buy anything from your company.

I trust that we shall not hear from Mr Higgins again, nor any other representative from your company.

Yours sincerely

David Rex
Director

MAKING COMPLAINTS – USING A STRONGER TONE
Letter 34: Letter of complaint about the quality of a product

If a supplier suddenly goes very quiet following a complaint you need to try to open the channels of communication again.

Although it will be irritating to you, and you may be feeling very annoyed, your letter should retain a tone of calm professionalism. There will be plenty of time to vent your feelings later. Your goal now is to force the supplier to respond. Reminding him that you are withholding payment should be sufficient to make him react.

SIMPSON
& MARTIN

39 TOP STREET
STOKE-ON-TRENT
ST2 3DR UNITED KINGDOM
Tel: (01782) 156232 Fax: (01782) 120899
Reg. No: England 96223978 VAT No: 91210674

Mr F Benson
Benson Envelopes
Unit 5 Longacre Ind. Est.
Stoke-on-Trent
ST5 7VB

30 August 1999

Dear Mr Benson

Our purchase order no. AB54673
I am extremely disappointed that I find myself having to write to you yet again.

I wrote to you on 9 August concerning a consignment of 50,000 C5 envelopes (printed one colour on front only) which we received from you on 6 August. A copy of my letter is enclosed. I remind you that we are withholding payment as the goods are defective.

Since then, a week has passed and I have received no reply from you, nor the replacement envelopes. I have telephoned several times but my calls have not been returned.

Please telephone me on receipt of this letter, to let me know when we can expect to receive the replacement order.

Yours sincerely

Vera Young
Marketing Production Manager

MAKING COMPLAINTS – USING A STRONGER TONE
Letter 35: Complaining about a service that fell well below acceptable standards

The disasters relayed in this letter reach the status of a catastrophe. Presenting the individual complaints as a list makes them appear far worse. Each one has been identified and will have to be accounted for. No amount of apology could undo the wrong. The strength of feeling is conveyed in the evocative phrase "shambolic disaster".

Hotels and restaurants live by their reputations and the manager will be well aware of the damage if his receives a bad name. He may not be too concerned if the writer doesn't eat there again but he will be concerned if lots of people are deterred from trying out the hotel.

PARKER
Glass Ltd
Unit 27 Willow Park
Christchurch, Dorset BH23 6MM
Tel: 01202 109111
Fax: 01202 109112

Reg. No: England 962578762
VAT No: 9120564

Mr P Hoat
Manager
Wayside Hotel
Riverside Walk
Christchurch
Dorset
BO4 2DD

24 July 1999

Dear Mr Hoat

Lunch at the Wayside Hotel on 23 July
Yesterday, I entertained three very important potential clients at your hotel, which, as your staff will confirm, I have visited on many occasions over the last two years.

It gives me no pleasure to say that the occasion was a shambolic disaster from start to finish.

1. It took a full fifteen minutes from placing our drinks order to being served with them - not a pleasant experience when all of us were parched.

2. We were not invited to take our seat in the dining room for a full 45 minutes after arriving.

3. The cold soup was spiced to a degree that was unbearable. No warning was given of this either in the menu or by the waiter.

4. One of the starters did not arrive until ten minutes after the others were served.

5. There was an unacceptable gap of 20 minutes between our finishing the starters and the main course arriving.

6. Two of the waiters, although not discourteous, did not show the attentiveness that is expected from a hotel of your class.

Had I realised that we would receive this kind of treatment I would not have entertained such important guests at your hotel. You have my assurance that I will not be entertaining or recommending anyone to eat there in future.

Yours sincerely

Frank Crasson

MAKING COMPLAINTS – USING A STRONGER TONE
Letter 36: Complaining that a verbal assurance has been broken

A verbal assurance is still a contract and one that here has been broken. The letter veers towards an angry tone when it uses the phrase "I was astounded..." but elsewhere retains its sense of measured annoyance.

Good phrases to remember to use when an agreement has been breached is the one: "...failure to comply with our terms..." and "...seeking recompense for any losses that we incur." It should be sufficient to put the wind up them.

 Kelso Limited
16 Abbots Road, Luton, Bedford MK44 7YT
Tel: (01234) 136953 Fax: (01234) 136422
Registered in England No: 9126719 VAT No: 91523489 76

Mr Hardy
Sales Manager
Cambridge Cutters Ltd
Gratton Road
Cambridge
CB1 1MJ

2 December 1999

Dear Mr Hardy

Our order no. 64987
I was given your verbal assurance on Tuesday that you would have no problem in completing the cutting processes requested for the folder order placed with you last week and delivering them to us on the Wednesday, in time for us to complete our processes. The order was booked in well in advance and we delivered the items to you at the time agreed.

I was therefore astounded to find that not only had you not completed the processes and returned the order to us by yesterday, but that we were not kept informed why the order would not be completed on time.

As your failure to comply with our terms will mean that our client will seek compensation from us for untimely delivery, we shall deduct any losses that we incur from your invoice.

Yours sincerely

John Piggott
Sales Director

MAKING COMPLAINTS – USING A STRONGER TONE
Letter 37: Firm letter to a supplier over a dispute

Here is an abundance of effective phrases to use in situations where you want to be firm about an issue: "...not of merchantable quality..."; "...don't have a moral leg to stand upon..."; "...really should know better..."; "...It was not we who caused this problem..."; "It is time this matter was brought to a close"; "...in full and final settlement...". These are all strong phrases that add weight to the claim being made and will convince the other side that you mean business.

Thomas King
& Palmer Ltd
serving the world

24 Fuller Road, Welling,
Kent DA16 7JP
Tel : (01322) 100132
Fax : (01322) 100178

Reg. No : England 1212298762
VAT No : 92905643

Mr S K Robinson
Sales Director
Wright & Robinson Ltd
43 Knights Drive
Kenilworth
Warwickshire
CV10 4ZN

13 June 1999

Dear Mr Robinson,

Our Purchase Order No. 346987; your Invoice No. 120786
Re your fax to our accounts manager of 10th April, regarding the dispute on this transaction, I shall deal with this matter. I am very sorry that you find yourself in the middle of this dispute.

As you know, quite simply, the list of names was not of merchantable quality as presented.

As you are also aware, the timings on mailings are always tight. Every mailer has to commit to print before the lists can be run. The stark alternative to reworking the list to make as much of it as possible mailable was to dump the mailing pieces prepared for the list. We would have needed a great deal more than a full credit to compensate for that. Re-working the list was the only option.

The list suppliers may not like our solution, but they do not have a moral leg to stand on. A list in this condition simply should not have been represented as a mailing list. As a regular mailer of international lists, we know what constitutes acceptable product, and this clearly did not. The list suppliers really should know better than to maintain that the original list rental should be paid in full. It was not we who caused this problem.

It is time this matter was brought to a close. We have always explained we are willing to pay the balance. Our final offer is therefore £112.55 + VAT in full and final settlement, made up as on the attached sheet. We will pay this on receipt of the credit note for £708.77 + VAT.

I look forward to hearing from you.

Yours sincerely

Arthur French
Marketing Director

MAKING COMPLAINTS – USING A STRONGER TONE
Letter 38: Stern reply to a negative response regarding a refund

Occasionally, a supplier will not play ball and may attempt to put up a fight. He may have decided (for whatever reason) that your business is not worth retaining.

Matters here are coming to a head. The supplying company is attempting to wriggle out of the complaint, but the customer is having none of it and knows that the law is on its side.

The phrase "we have now decided to take legal advice...with a view to recovery of our money..." and "...instructions will be issued to our solicitors to proceed against you" are designed to leave the supplier in no doubt that he must pay up or face legal action.

GKT Products Ltd, Unit 10, Castleway Lane, Alloway, Ayr, KA7 4BE
Telephone (01292) 177900 Fax (01292) 199855   Reg. No: 17964583 VAT No: 679845

Mr Paul Newman
Marketing Executive
Computer & Stationery Supplies
Parkside Business Park
Oakham
Leicester
LE4 7HJ

28 April 1999

Dear Mr Newman

Our order 219784
I refer to your letter of 23rd April 1999 about a consignment of faulty computer disks that we received from you on April 5th.

In your letter you claim that these disks are of the highest quality and would, therefore, have left your premises in perfect condition. You presume, therefore, that they must have been mishandled in some way by us and that the fault is, therefore, ours. You also state that these disks were supplied at a special promotional discount and that discounted goods are not subject to replacement or refund. This point, you maintain, would have been made clear to us at the time of purchase.

I must point out to you that we have many years experience and our staff are highly trained and know very well how to handle and store computer disks. We can assure you that these disks **were** faulty at the time we received them. We do not doubt your company's ability to handle such equipment but feel particularly aggrieved that you feel free to doubt ours. On this point alone, we have decided to have no more dealings with your company.

On the matter of the special promotional discount, you can be assured that at no time was any caveat given to us regarding refunds. You will also be aware that the Sale of Goods Act 1979 states quite clearly that faulty goods **are** subject to refund or replacement. A simple disclaimer on your part does not alter the law in any way.

We have now decided to take legal advice on this matter, with a view to recovery of our money and you are advised that, unless a full refund is received from you within three days, instructions will be issued to our solicitors to proceed against you.

As stated, we will be having no further dealings with your company.

Yours sincerely,

Betty Davis
Purchasing Manager

Managing customers

Chapter 2
Managing customers

The customer is king. But knowing that doesn't make it any easier when you have an awkward one to manage, or mistakes happen that need to be sorted out. There can be few matters less pleasant than an irate customer, and few more gratifying than one who is satisfied. The letters in this chapter provide a wealth of ideas for keeping relations with customers on an even keel and, when the waters turn choppy, what you can do to calm them down again.

Saying sorry

It sounds simple, but how many customers genuinely believe what you say? Saying sorry sincerely, so that a customer decides to stay with you rather than move to your competition, is an art. Letters 56 and 57 are examples of those that genuinely worked.

What if they are trying it on?

Sometimes, you may find yourself up against a customer who is being economical with the truth. You can't openly accuse them of lying, so how do you handle it? Letter 58 shows how.

Handling awkward customers

Difficult customers need to be handled carefully. Don't just ignore them even if they are rude, as in letter 59. And don't let them steamroller their way with you – be firm, as in letter 61.

The easiest source of new business?

Your existing customers are your easiest source of new business. They have used you once and, if they enjoyed the experience, they will come back to you again, and again. Taking the time and trouble to thank them may not seem a profitable use of your time but it will reap rewards. Letters 66–70 give plenty of ideas.

Don't forget your lapsed customers

These ones are well worth trying to revive. You won't get them all back, but just a few will make the effort worthwhile. See letters 73 and 75.

GIVING QUOTATIONS
Letter 39: Providing a quote, ex-works

'Ex-works' is a term that commonly occurs in quotations and means that the supplier makes the goods available from his premises. Unless stated otherwise, the purchaser is expected to arrange collection of the goods and organise any export licences and other documentation that may be required, as well as transportation. The purchaser assumes the full risk of damage to the goods, once the goods are in his control. For a precise understanding of the term ex-works (and other shipping terms), it is recommended that you consult a copy of the Incoterms which can be obtained from the International Chamber of Commerce,
tel. 0171-823 2811.

Note again, the helpful advice that the supplier is giving: what additional costs will have to be borne; the fact it will be cheaper to transport the items by sea rather than air and when he is going to be unavailable.

⊛ WILSON SMITH LTD
A wholly-owned subsidiary of The Wilson Group PLC
16 Willow Walk, Retford, Nottingham NG6 8WS
Tel: (01777) 121211 Fax: (01777) 121233
Reg. No: England 1212298762

Mr Winston Pathmanathan
Director
Kuantan Industries
5 Ipoh Street
5100 Kuala Lumpur
Malaysia

20 July 1999

Dear Winston

I am pleased to quote you ex-works prices for the items, as requested. All are in excellent working order but, in some cases, I am offering you an alternative for new items. I cannot give you the total price until I know exactly what you require, as we will have to add inland haulage, packing and freight charges. Please let me know whether you want the items sent by sea or air freight. Given the bulk of some of them, sea would be cheaper.

1. Photocopiers @ £940.00 each.

2. IBM Typewriters - second-hand Golf Ball @ £90.00 each. New modern electronic @ £360.00 each.

3. Olympia manual typewriters - second-hand @ £105.00 each. New @ £300.00 each.

4. Fax machines - we can supply new or reconditioned second-hand @ £375.00 each. Obviously, the second-hand ones are sturdier machines with more functions than the new ones for the same price.

Please contact me as soon as possible, to let me know your requirements as I shall be away on annual leave for two weeks from 6th – 23rd August.

I look forward to hearing from you shortly.

Yours sincerely,

James Smith
Marketing Director

This quotation is to a customer who the supplier already knows. It doesn't have the formality of a quotation form. The supplier knows that the customer probably doesn't wants more than 100kg and so doesn't bother to provide the figures, but leaves the option open. He also ends the letter confidently, expecting the order.

Note how the supplier is using his skill to advise the customer on what he believes will be the best option, given the specification that has been asked for. This kind of service will be appreciated, and the customer may be more inclined to place an order, because he knows his requirements will be looked after.

If the customer had to choose between one supplier who offered a straight quote and this supplier who is offering a quote and helpful advice, it is easy to see which one he is likely to opt for.

WILSON SMITH LTD

A wholly-owned subsidiary of The Wilson Group PLC
16 Willow Walk, Retford, Nottingham NG6 8WS
Tel: (01777) 121211 Fax: (01777) 121233
Reg. No: England 1212298762

Mr G Benn
Sales Manager
Drake & Huggins Ltd
Orchard Road
Saffron Walden
Essex
CB21 6HN

19 August 1999

Dear Gordon,

I confirm our faxed quotation for yellow ruling powder at £6.00 per kg. If you require more than 100kg, we can offer you better prices.

I enclose the standard colour range. Please note that, although, we are able to produce a lemon yellow, this appears rather dull. I have therefore excluded it, as I believe your client specified it should be bright. Also, the royal blue and black print up much more strongly than in the sample shown, as these prints have been produced on the wrong paper. I am getting some more drawn up on the correct substrate and will forward them to you as soon as they are available.

I look forward to hearing from you and, of course, to receiving your order.

Yours sincerely,

John Wilson
Sales Director

Here a situation has arisen, where a quoted price is significantly lower than it is in reality. The difference is so great that the customer may already realise it is a simple typographical error. Nevertheless, the supplier wants to retain the goodwill of the customer.

Making light of it in this way is not always appropriate: it all depends on how well you know your customer. Here, they get on very well, so the tone is fitting.

Passing the blame on to an imaginary 'gremlin' also cleverly diverts the attention away from the real cause of the mistake – yourself, perhaps.

The exclamation mark in brackets in the last sentence lightens what might otherwise be a rather solemn sentence.

BELLS OF BASILDON

Bells of Basildon Ltd, Unit 12, Way Park, Basildon SS12 6DE
Tel: 01268 109 9954 Fax: 01268 109 5576 Reg. No. England 13078453 VAT No: 75698764

Mr J Bracket
Purchasing Manager
A S Charlwood Ltd
87 Main Street
Brentwood
Essex
CH7 8DC

16 June 1999

Dear Jim

What can I say? Sorry.

It seems a gremlin got into our wordprocessor and decided to move the decimal point over a little too far. The price should of course have been £2545 and not £254.50. We are doing our best to control the beast but it still occasionally steps out of line.

I hope, in spite of the apparent tenfold increase (!), that the price is still acceptable.

Yours sincerely

Terry Monk
Estimator

A supplier here has misquoted a price. It may be that the customer thought he was going to be getting a bargain of a better model at a lower price. The customer's reaction is bound to be one of disappointment, especially as he is being asked to pay almost another £200.

The supplier, concerned that this may be enough to deter the customer, works hard to retain the business by taking the opportunity of pointing out the additional features of the more expensive model.

To draw the sting of the higher price the supplier offers a nice surprise to the customer – a small free item, which will go a long way towards retaining the goodwill of the customer, which will far outweigh the cost of the pointer.

H J KINGSLEY (NORWICH) LTD
Kingsley House, Morris Street, Norwich NR6 7JM
Tel: (01603) 117097 Fax: (01603) 117099 Reg. No: England 12086215 VAT No: 8793519

Mr W Johns
General Manager
Gurteen & Parker
Unit 7 Meadowview Ind. Est.
Norwich
NR2 4ED

15 February 1999

Dear Mr Johns

Nobo 90 Overhead Projector
Thank you for your letter querying the price of the Nobo 90 Overhead Projector.

I confirm the price of this item is £595 (excluding VAT) and not £409 as previously stated. It seems that the person who took your original call misheard the model number. I apologise for this error. However, as I am sure you have already discovered, the Nobo 99 has the advantages of being both more compact and lighter than the Nobo 90, as well as having better-quality lenses. All Nobo models come with a 12-month, on-site guarantee.

I am sorry if this oversight has caused you any inconvenience. As a token of our appreciation of your custom, we are pleased to offer you a free telescopic pointer with your order.

Yours sincerely

Marilyn Morris
Sales Director

RESPONDING TO ENQUIRIES AND ORDERS
Letter 43: Welcoming a new customer, informally

Too many businesses take new customers for granted, even though they are like gold dust.

A letter of welcome should take the opportunity to give the customer the confidence that she has chosen the right company and is in safe hands.

Note how the business creates a good impression in the mind of the customer, by offering an additional service free of charge as a 'nice surprise'.

Expressions worth noting here are: "...a long and happy association..." and "...should we fall short of your high expectations...", which emphasise how much trouble your business is prepared to take to help and leaves the customer feeling comfortable with choosing you.

IDENDEN INDUSTRIES
A division of Idenden Plc
Porter House, Hull HU7 4RF England

Tel 01482 119087 Fax 01482 119088
Registered in England No: 1218943

Mrs J Holmes
Holmes and Barker Associates
23 Holly Bush Lane
Stretham
Cambs
CB8 4JK

16 August 1999

Dear Mrs Holmes

Interior fittings for 23 Holly Bush Lane
Many thanks for your order received today.

We are delighted that you have chosen us to supply you with interior fittings for your new premises. I hope that you will be pleased with the results of our work but, should you have any quibble, however small, please contact me and I will ensure that it is attended to immediately.

As part of our welcome pack for new clients, your order entitles you to have a free consultation, with a recommendation of how the workspace can be designed to the ergonomic advantage of your employees. This service is completely free to all customers placing their first order with us before the end of the year. If you would like to take advantage of this limited offer, please complete and return the enclosed card.

We look forward to a long and happy association with your business. Should we fall short of your high expectations in any matter, please contact me personally.

Yours sincerely

Stuart Jones
Sales Manager

Taking the trouble to welcome a new customer is a good opportunity to offer thanks for their custom.

Here, the business has to get the customer to sign an agreement – potentially tricky, as it is an opportunity for the customer to decide they don't want your service after all.

Instead of stressing that the customer is now committing herself to the agreement, the writer cunningly puts himself into the shoes of the customer, when he says these are "...our promises 'and your rights'..." a careful choice of phrase, designed to make the customer feel like a winner.

Note also how the process is made to seem so easy "...simply sign both copies...".

IDENDEN INDUSTRIES
A division of Idenden Plc
Porter House, Hull HU7 4RF England

Tel 01482 119087 Fax 01482 119088
Registered in England No: 1218943

Mrs J Holmes
Holmes and Barker Associates
23 Holly Bush Lane
Stretham
Cambs
CB8 4JK

16 August 1999

Dear Mrs Holmes

Your order no: BYR 99854WE
Thank you for your order.

We have arranged for an engineer to call at your premises to fit your boiler on the morning of the 6 September 1999, if this is convenient for you.

We note that you have opted for our full-service agreement to cover maintenance of the boiler and any spare parts. I enclose a service agreement, listing the conditions under which maintenance and parts will be supplied, together with a copy of our 12 months-guarantee, which sets out our promises (and your rights if we fail to live up to any of them).

Please check all the details. If you are happy with them, simply sign both copies of the agreement and return one to us in the return envelope provided.

If you have any queries, please do not hesitate to call us on 01482 119087, from 9am to 5pm, Monday to Saturday.

We look forward to welcoming you as a customer.

Yours sincerely

Robert Patterson
Account Manager

Just occasionally, you may find yourself in the happy position of having two customers competing for the same item, as here. It may not happen very often but it can do wonders for concentrating the customer's mind on the buying decision.

Here, the supplier signals that he is going to accept the highest bidder. A word of warning though, don't play this game unless you have someone else who is seriously interested -- otherwise it could backfire on you badly. You should also bear in mind that the loser may feel ill will towards you. If you think a longer-term relationship may be jeopardised, it would be better to accept the first offer and tell the second client that the item is already sold.

⊛ WILSON SMITH LTD

A wholly-owned subsidiary of The Wilson Group PLC
16 Willow Walk, Retford, Nottingham NG6 8WS
Tel: (01777) 121211 Fax: (01777) 121233
Reg. No: England 1212298762

Mr Winston Pathmanathan
Director
Kuantan Industries
5 Ipoh Street
5100 Kuala Lumpur
Malaysia

30 November 1999

Dear Winston

Re Chambon machine
As requested, I enclose the specification and photograph of the Chambon machine, which we have on offer.

We currently have a potential buyer from Ghana, who is interested and has offered £50,000 ex-works. We are prepared to accept this offer and he will be looking at the machine next week, unless you are seriously interested and make a better offer. Please 'phone or fax me quickly, before I close the deal with this client.

I look forward to hearing from you.

Yours sincerely,

John Wilson
Sales Director

Occasionally, customers may place an order but omit a fundamental piece of information or, as here, misunderstand how many items are in a packet. The more technical the item being requested, the more likely this is to occur.

Here, the supplier is asking the customer to confirm what is required. It can be dangerous to make assumptions about an order when it is not clear. The last thing this supplier would want to do is to send out the wrong items and find them coming flooding back, especially when the customer is being asked to pay in advance of receiving the items.

Don't forget, even if the customer is in the wrong, it still puts you in a bad light.

⊛ WILSON SMITH LTD

A wholly-owned subsidiary of The Wilson Group PLC
16 Willow Walk, Retford, Nottingham NG6 8WS
Tel: (01777) 121211 Fax: (01777) 121233
Reg. No: England 1212298762

Mr Winston Pathmanathan
Director
Kuantan Industries
5 Ipoh Street
5100 Kuala Lumpur
Malaysia

8 February 1999

Dear Winston,

Many thanks for your letter of 13th January.

Unfortunately, I think you have made a number of errors in your request, which has prevented me from sending you the pro forma invoices.

1. On all the plates you have requested 'Packets'. SORD, KORD AND ROLAND plates are packed 25 per packet and M1850 and G201 are 100 per packet. This would mean, for example, 1,250 KORD plates costing $6,787.50 and 5,000 1850 plates costing $7,250.00. If this is correct, your total consignment would cost about $65,000.

2. There are two sizes of ROLAND 3 plate, as specified in my letter of 15th October. Which size is required?

3. Do you require Negative or Positive plates for M1850 and GTO?

I would be grateful if you could answer these queries by return, so that we can process your order for you as soon as possible.

Yours sincerely,

James Smith
Marketing Director

RESPONDING TO ENQUIRIES AND ORDERS
Letter 47: Acknowledging an order – goods temporarily out of stock

This is a courteous, standard letter, notifying that an item on an order is out of stock. It doesn't have a personalised ring to it. The clue to this is that the title is not mentioned in the letter, only on the invoice. And no reference is made to the way the customer has actually paid – it says what happens depending on how he has paid.

A hint of personal attention comes through in the second paragraph, where a promise is made to be in contact if the order cannot be supplied within two weeks. Another nice touch is shown in giving a 'phone number to ring if there is a problem. This is on the letterhead anyway, but it makes the number easier to find and subtly reassures the customer.

Grange & Turner Ltd
32 WESTBOURN ROAD, WITNEY, OXON OX6 7HY

Telephone (01993) 107888
Fax (01993) 107843

Reg. No: England 13078453
VAT No: 75698764

15 St Patricks Road
Cottingham
Hull
HU5 3SR

12 August 1999

Dear Mr Black,

Your order 134987
Thank you for your recent order. I am afraid that we have temporarily sold out of the title indicated on the invoice.

New stocks have already been ordered and we expect delivery shortly. Of course, I will contact you again if I cannot despatch your book within the next two weeks.

If you have paid in advance, your cheque will not be banked until we have despatched all the items on your order. If you have paid by credit card, we will only debit for those items you have received so far.

All our books are supplied under our usual 10-day examination offer. If you have any further questions please do not hesitate to ring me on 01993 107888.

Please accept my apologies for this delay.

Your sincerely

Kevin Mason
General Manager

RESPONDING TO ENQUIRIES AND ORDERS
Letter 48: Telling a customer it's too late to amend an order

A customer has made a mistake with an order and the supplier is responding. The supplier gives the buyer an option to amend part of the order as they are only part way through the job.

The supplier's reply is courteous and to the point. It could have taken a tougher line saying 'you *must* accept the 150 ringbinders already made'. Instead it takes the softer approach of "...we will have to ask you..." as he knows the customer is in the wrong and there is no need to add insult to injury.

RPP Holdings Plc
35/38 New Road, Paignton, Devon TQ3 4UU
Tel: 01803 175653 Fax: 01803 187908
Reg. No: England 1976143

FAX MESSAGE

To: Tom Greate
          Wilson Smith Ltd

Fax No: 01777 121233

From: Bob Taylor   Date: 22 February 1999

Dear Tom,

Your order no 30596
I received your fax this morning, requesting that your order for 500 ringbinders with a 30mm diameter ring be amended to binders that take 350 leaves.

Unfortunately, your order has already been in production for two days and we have made up 150 ringbinders. As these have been tailored to your requirements with your company's logo, we will have to ask you to accept the 150 ringbinders already made.

Please let me know today if you want a further 500 ringbinders with a 35mm diameter ring made or just 350.

Yours sincerely

Bob Taylor
Sales Manager

Unwanted mail can be a major source of irritation – mainly to consumers. Businesses seem to accept more readily that it is part and parcel of their daily life. With most respectable companies, it should be possible to restrict the amount of direct mail you receive, simply by asking to be taken off their mailing lists.

This letter reassures the recipient that appropriate action is being taken. Note how it opens, thanking the customer for taking the trouble to write: a nice way of disarming a complainant.

The letter doesn't grovel but points out exactly what the person can expect to happen and it offers a course of action if things don't improve and reminds the consumer that it is in the company's interests, ultimately, to keep mailings down – something the person writing in would not think about automatically.

Grange & Turner Ltd

32 WESTBOURN ROAD, WITNEY, OXON OX6 7HY

Telephone (01993) 107888
Fax (01993) 107843

Reg. No: England 13078453
VAT No: 75698764

Mr P Brooks
33 Little Lane
East Bridgford
Nottingham
NG55 6YH

16 May 1999

Dear Mr Brooks

Thank you for taking the trouble to write, asking for your name to be removed from our mailing list. From today, your name and address will be excluded from all mailing lists produced here.

I should warn you that most mailings are prepared a long way in advance and it is almost certain that some are yet to be posted. I can only apologise for the irritation these further mailings may cause but please be assured that they will soon come to a stop.

However, if they cause you concern, and you would like me to carry out an additional check, simply return the unwanted letter using our FREEPOST address:

Jane Harvey
List Controller
Grange & Turner Ltd
FREEPOST
Witney
OX6 7HY

We are always keen to keep our mailing costs down, wherever possible, and to mail only those who wish to hear from us.

If you have any further questions please do not hesitate to contact me.

Yours sincerely

Jane Harvey
List Controller

The customer writing in obviously appreciates the service being offered and the tone of the letter fits the degree of the complaint. If there is a hint of good news in the complainant's letter it is well worth latching on to it, as here. It helps to remove some of the sting and put your company into a more positive light.

You still want to remedy the situation and, provided that you can take action or be seen to be taking action to satisfy the customer, you should not be troubled in the future.

Grange & Turner Ltd

32 WESTBOURN ROAD, WITNEY, OXON OX6 7HY

Telephone (01993) 107888
Fax (01993) 107843

Reg. No: England 13078453
VAT No: 75698764

Mr H Mason
15 Longfield Road
Boars Hill
Oxford
OX568JH

24 February 1999

Dear Mr Mason,

Thank you for your letter dated 17th February addressed to our Managing Director, which has been brought to my attention. It is very nice to hear that you appreciate receiving our promotional material from time to time.

However, I am very sorry that you have been inundated with mailings to your son at your address. This has happened because he requested us to send goods to your address as above; with hindsight, we should have made sure that our computer was "flagged" no mailings on his name.

I would like to confirm that we have amended our records so that he will only receive his mailings at his Leighton Buzzard address and have arranged that only our literature is sent in future. You may receive unwanted mailings for about a month as there may be some in the pipeline but, after that period of time, they should stop.

Once again, please accept my apologies for the annoyance and inconvience caused. If you have any more queries please do not hesitate to contact me.

Yours sincerely

Jane Harvey
List Controller

The company complaining about the poor service here believes that the cleaning company has ignored its first letter, even though it seems that it has genuinely gone astray. This is unfortunate, because it means the writer will have to work doubly hard to convince the customer that the fault is completely innocent. This is successfully achieved here.

Being seen to do more than is strictly required is a useful tactic for handling complaints. Here, the cleaning company takes the precaution of allocating a new person to the job and offering a discount off the month's invoice.

Be modest also in the extent to which you claim to be compensating the other party. Note how the writer says "...and trust that this *helps in* compensating for your dissatisfaction". He could have written "...and trust this compensates you for your dissatisfaction", which would appear slightly presumptuous and probably negate all the profuse apologies that have been made.

BAKER CLEANING SERVICES

29 Cunningham Street
London
N32 6JG
Telephone: (0171) 016 1350
Facsimile: (0171) 016 1351

Reg. No: England 118974165

Mrs E Bjornsen
General Manager
Hansoms Auctions
153 Simpson Street
London
WC3 4RT

10 July 1999

Dear Mrs Bjornsen,

Thank you for your letter of the 5th July, expressing concern over the cleaning service that we provide for your company.

You say that you have written to us once already on this matter but, having looked into this, we can find no record of ever having received your letter. We are not sure what happened here but we very much regret that this has meant a continuation of your problem.

In your letter, you state that toilet areas are not adequately cleaned or disinfected and that the office area, although always vacuumed properly, is often not dusted or polished.

I have spoken to the four staff who clean your offices on a rota and I believe I have now isolated the problem. Although the cause seems to have arisen out of a temporary problem affecting one of our cleaners, I have taken the precaution of assigning a permanent replacement to your team and I have reminded all cleaners that only the highest standards are acceptable.

I very much regret the inconvenience and disappointment caused and hope that the measures taken will now restore the service we offer to its former high standard. As a token of our goodwill, I have arranged for a discount of 30% off this month's invoice and trust that this helps in compensating for your dissatisfaction.

Once again, please accept our sincerest apologies.

Yours sincerely,

Jill Hooper
Account Manager

When you are relying on a distributor or wholesaler for a product who in turn is relying on the main supplier overseas to supply an item, it is easy to find yourself the piggy in the middle between a customer and the people who can influence getting the product to you.

Obtaining reliable information about time-scales or delivery through the chain of suppliers is often difficult. When this occurs, your main line of defence with the customer has to be that you are applying pressure as regularly as possible.

H J KINGSLEY (NORWICH) LTD

Kingsley House, Morris Street, Norwich NR6 7JM
Tel: (01603) 117097 Fax: (01603) 117099 Reg. No: England 12086215 VAT No: 8793519

Mr F Goodge
Goodge, Turner and Weatherall
12 Macers Row
Holt
Norfolk
NR16 5TR

12 February 1999

Dear Mr Goodge

Axe accounting package

I am sorry that you have still not received this software package.

It is an American import which is distributed by a UK software house and there is a delay in getting stocks from the States. We are nagging the UK software house twice a week, who assure us that they are doing the same to their American colleagues.

I will keep you informed of progress.

Yours sincerely

Anne Goode (Mrs)
Sales Assistant

The two people who were due to meet know each other well. Even though one of them has been inconvenienced, the tone is friendly, fitting their established relationship. Bob knows that Andrew Taylor is to be trusted and doesn't make a habit of missing appointments. If they had not known each other, a much more formal tone would be called for.

Even though the letter is friendly, note how the feeling is still sincere – Andrew empathises with Bob saying: "I know how frustrating it is to be left high and dry..." A recompense is offered in the form of a lunch. Another highlighting device is used with the PS – here Andrew wants to confirm that he really means June and has not made another mistake.

Taylor Taylor & Shaw

Benton House, Clifton, Bristol BS16 7LJ
Tel: (0117) 1089254   Fax: (0117) 1089211

Mr R Hodds
Director
RLO (of Bristol) Ltd
32 Gloucester Road
Clifton
Bristol
BS8 4UP

14 June 1999

Dear Bob

I am very sorry that you were left waiting at your offices for the meeting that we had arranged last week.

I know how frustrating it is to be left high and dry and I take all the blame for getting it wrong. I wrote your appointment down for 13 July instead of 13 June.

To make amends, can I offer you lunch when we meet? How are you fixed for 18 June at 12 o'clock? I suggest we meet at my office, if that is convenient to you.

Yours sincerely

Andrew W Taylor

PS I really do mean June this time!

Partners: AW Taylor & GS Taylor

Here, there is not a serious complaint, although the customer has noticed that goods are taking longer to arrive. The fault lies outside the direct control of the supplying company although it is within its power to amend, as it is the courier whose service has deteriorated.

The tone is conciliatory, without treating the situation as a big problem. "We are, of course, concerned...." is another useful phrase, helping to create the impression that you empathise with the reader and recognise the problem.

⊗ WILSON SMITH LTD
A wholly-owned subsidiary of The Wilson Group PLC
16 Willow Walk, Retford, Nottingham NG6 8WS
Tel: (01777) 121211 Fax: (01777) 121233
Reg. No: England 1212298762

Mr J West
General Manager
Idenden Industries
Porter House
Hull
HU7 4RF

16 May 1999

Dear Jim

Re: Delivery times
Thank you for returning the delivery cards: showing how long it is taking for our goods to arrive with you.

Your observation that deliveries seem to be taking longer than a year ago is correct. On average it is taking one extra day for goods to arrive with you, although our overall turnaround time from receiving your order to goods leaving the warehouse has not changed.

The cause of this extra time seems be the courier service we are currently using. We are, of course, concerned to offer you the best possible service, so for the next three months we shall be trying out an alternative service, to see if there is any improvement.

Please do continue to return the cards showing the date you receive the goods and please accept our sincere apologies for this slight deterioration in service.

Yours sincerely

Peter Grey
General Manager

A customer may specify that a product must meet certain criteria. Unfortunately, he may not appreciate that meeting those criteria could have a knock-on effect elsewhere. Here the customer wants the inks to be tolerant of high temperatures *and* retain their glossy appearance. The key phrase here is "...I assure you this is perfectly normal and will not impede its function". "I trust everything is in order..." is a useful phrase to use when you are confident that what you are suggesting should satisfy the reader, but it still leaves the door open if they have any more queries.

 WILSON SMITH LTD

A wholly-owned subsidiary of The Wilson Group PLC
16 Willow Walk, Retford, Nottingham NG6 8WS
Tel: (01777) 121211 Fax: (01777) 121233
Reg. No: England 1212298762

Mr Brian Adams
Production Director
FGH Products Ltd
Unit 8 Potters Lane Ind. Est.
Almondvale
Perth
PH1 2EL

29 September 1999

Dear Mr Adams,

Many thanks for the cheque for £394.00 received this morning, and I understand the reason for the delay in this payment.

I note that you were unhappy with the quality of some of the materials we sent and I would like to explain the situation. Your order specified that the product should be tolerant of high temperatures. The gloss version has a lower tolerance, which is why we supplied the matt to you. This is why the product may appear slightly rough although I assure you this is perfectly normal and will not impede its function.

I trust everything is in order and I look forward to being able to provide further quotations for you in the future.

Yours sincerely

Mike Rose
Sales Department

APOLOGIES WITH A HINT OF GROVELLING
Letter 56: Apologising for breaking a verbal assurance

Letters that explain the reason for a mistake can give the customer an impression that you are being very defensive in passing the buck on to someone else instead of accepting responsibility for your actions. This can reduce still further the customer's estimation of you, rather than restoring his faith in your ability to deliver the services. This letter tackles this issue nicely in the second paragraph, with the phrase "If I could perhaps explain the circumstances, not as an excuse, but so you can see the exceptional...".

The sincerity of this letter is emphasised by the phrases "I was most disturbed..."; "...and I am deeply sorry..." and "This unfortunate event...". And it is not just simple apologies the reader is being asked to accept, but "unreserved" apologies. The use of these emphatic words builds up a greater sense of remorse.

RPP Holdings Plc
35/38 New Road, Paignton, Devon TQ3 4UU
Tel: 01803 175653 Fax: 01803 187908
Reg. No: England 1976143

Mr P Piggott
Managing Director
TMP UK Ltd
Manor Park
Hitchin
Herts
HP7 9UM

23 April 1999

Dear Mr Piggott

I was most disturbed to receive your letter of 20 April, informing me of your dissatisfaction with our performance. I am deeply sorry that we have let you and your client down. We take great care to ensure that our customers are satisfied, as this is essential to the continuation of our business.

If I could perhaps explain the circumstances, not as an excuse but so you can see the exceptional and unexpected difficulties we faced. When I telephoned you on Tuesday, your order was on track to be supplied the following day. Soon after we spoke, I had to leave the factory for an unavoidable meeting. An hour later, the machine developed a fault which took four hours to rectify and this meant we were unable to complete your order. Because I was expected back the same day, it was left for me to telephone you to explain the situation. By bad luck, I was detained longer than expected and did not return to the factory the same day.

This unfortunate event has highlighted a gap in our procedures, which we are correcting. In future, in my absence, our Production Manager will notify you of any deviation from the agreed schedule.

Please accept our unreserved apologies. We shall, subject to documentary proof, of course, make good any losses that you incur as a result of our failure to meet your deadline.

Yours sincerely

JH Hardy
Customer Services Manager

APOLOGIES WITH A HINT OF GROVELLING
Letter 57: Apologising to a customer for items that have not arrived

When a customer complains, it is not just the current order that you may lose. That customer could be worth a lot of money to you over time – accounting for thousands of pounds of revenue during the time he does business with you.

If mistakes do happen your aim should be to mitigate the damage. Here, the supplier achieves this by reassuring the customer that it is a "...very rare occurrence...", supporting the claim with "...it happens about once a year...".

The customer is made to feel extra-special, with the remedy of having the item sent by special delivery, being referred to as a "...highly valued customer..." and being given a voucher for a discount off the next purchase – a cunning technique to tempt the customer back, which costs very little and boosts sales at the same time. Brilliant!

Grange & Turner Ltd

32 WESTBOURN ROAD, WITNEY, OXON OX6 7HY

Telephone (01993) 107888
Fax (01993) 107843

Reg. No: England 13078453
VAT No: 75698764

Mr W Holmes
154 High Road
Oakley
Oxford
OX7 8PL

21 June 1999

Dear Mr Holmes,

Re: The Power to Win

I was extremely concerned to hear that you have not received the above book, which should have been despatched to you a week ago.

I have made enquiries and have discovered that, in this instance, one of our internal procedural systems failed. This is a very rare occurrence (it happens about once a year although we continue to try to eradicate such mistakes entirely).

I can only ask that you accept our most sincere apologies for this inconvenience. To make amends, I am sending you a copy of the above book by special delivery. In addition, as you are a highly valued customer, I am enclosing a £5 voucher, which can be redeemed against any future order.

I do hope that this will go some way to restoring your faith in us.

Yours sincerely,

Susan Taylor
Customer Service Manager

Occasionally, you may come up against a situation where the facts just don't fit. You don't have the evidence to say: 'I don't believe you; you're lying', so how do you handle it? The simple business decision is to refuse to do business with the customer any more.

The supplier here produces the evidence that the goods are being delivered correctly and then in the third paragraph tells the customer that the supplier smells a rat with the phrases "...very odd indeed" and the fact that goods are "...apparently..." not being received safely. This gets as close to a specific challenge as you can afford.

The customer is the loser in the end, as he will now be blacklisted and unable to receive any more goods.

Grange & Turner Ltd

32 WESTBOURN ROAD, WITNEY, OXON OX6 7HY

Telephone (01993) 107888
Fax (01993) 107843

Reg. No: England 13078453
VAT No: 75698764

Mr T P Smith
124 Vale Road
Clifton
Bristol
BS5 7HY

24 July 1999

Dear Mr Smith,

Our Statement dated 12 April 1999

We have supplied you with books on four separate occasions to the value of £75, for which we have asked for payment three times.

You are claiming that you have never received the items ordered and that they must have been lost in the post. Our carrier's records demonstrate that the goods were despatched and each time signed for by a D M Martin. You claim that no one of that name lives at your address and that the goods must have been incorrectly delivered.

We could understand if a parcel was incorrectly delivered on one occasion but the fact that parcels have been delivered and accepted four times by the same person seems very odd indeed.

As our debt cannot be settled and goods supplied to this address are apparently not being received safely, we have no alternative but to cease fulfilling orders to you. We shall write off the amount of £75 on this occasion.

Yours sincerely

T P O'Neil
Customer Accounts Manager
Mr D Redwood
Cedar Cottage

HANDLING AWKWARD CUSTOMERS
Letter 59: Handling a very rude customer

Some people's reaction to receiving an abusive letter is to bin the letter, because it obviously comes from a crank. But wait a minute. That person isn't reacting for no reason at all – he obviously feels very strongly about the issue. And, since he has cast aspertions on the reputation of your business, you should use the opportunity to set the record straight.

The first sentence tackles the abusiveness head-on. The phrase "In spite of your rude tone I will respond..." is designed to make him feel that you almost decided not to write and that he should appreciate that you have taken the trouble.

Note how the tone of the reply is cold and unapologetic. It offers a frank explanation without saying either "sorry" or "please accept our apologies".

PARKER
Glass Ltd
Unit 27 Willow Park
Christchurch, Dorset BH23 6MM
Tel: 01202 109111
Fax: 01202 109112

Reg. No: England 962578762
VAT No: 9120564

Mr S Wright
157 Colder Way
Basingstoke
Hants
BP6 5TG

12 December 1999

Dear Mr Wright,

It is not often I receive such an offensive letter. In spite of your rude tone I will respond to the issues you raised.

I understand that your letter is caused by your frustration at not being supplied immediately with the goods that you ordered. We take great pride in being able to supply all goods *held in stock* within 28 days at the latest. Our average turnaround time is, however, far shorter, at just nine working days. But there are occasions, such as this instance, when the demand for our goods is much greater than we anticipate. Normally we would simply reorder and aim to supply you within about two weeks. However, when the goods have to be imported from overseas, delays can be considerably longer. These are the circumstances that caused you such offence.

We are doing everything in our power to obtain the goods and supply them to you. I would like to reassure you that we shall not deduct the amount owed from your credit card until the day the goods are despatched to you. We always take complaints seriously and are ready to respond to all of them. I accept you feel strongly about this situation, but I would ask that any future correspondence between us is conducted in more appropriate language.

Yours sincerely

Peter Jones
Managing Director

Sometimes, you may feel that a customer has completely ignored proper instructions. If you cave in to the complaint, you risk opening the flood gates to other unjustified complaints. A better course is to stand firm and politely point out that the product was not used for the purpose intended. After all, the product is being called into question and to offer any recompense may be interpreted as an admission that the product is at fault.

The evidence needs to be irrefutable, as here, when warnings are given in the instruction manual about which materials the drill is suitable for and which it is not. Note how the line of evidence is separated out from the rest of the text, since it is the crux of the argument. Emboldening it heightens the eye's attention to it. The door is shut firmly in the customer's face with the phrase "...I regret that we are unable to assist you further in this matter", a wonderfully polite and understated way of saying 'get lost' without causing offence.

IDENDEN INDUSTRIES
A division of Idenden Plc
Porter House, Hull HU7 4RF England

Tel 01482 119087 Fax 01482 119088
Registered in England No: 1218943

Little Lane
Wass
York
YO9 6TG

3 February 1999

Dear Mr Redwood,

I have considered your letter of 21st January and your assertion that our K31 power drill does not fulfil the claims made for it.

In your letter you maintain that this drill was used by you as directed, in the construction of a new extension to your house, as a result of which the motor burnt out only a month after the expiry of the guarantee. A telephone call to you from one of our staff subsequently revealed that you used this drill with a large masonry bit, for drilling into concrete.

I feel that I should point out that our K31 model is an *excellent* drill for the purposes for which it is sold, that is, for light jobs around the home. This point is made quite clearly in the instruction manual which come with your drill, in particular at the bottom of section two "Suitable Material" where it states:

"This drill is not suitable for heavy-duty drilling in materials such as concrete."

Much more suitable would be one of our K80 or K90 range, in that they have more robust motors as well as an impact facility, normally expected for drilling into materials such as concrete. The K31 boasts no such facility.

For these reasons I regret, therefore, that I cannot agree with your assertion.

Since your guarantee has expired, and since your drill has been used for purposes **specifically** stated as unsuitable, I regret that we are unable to assist you further in this matter.

Yours sincerely,

Frank Pillow
Customer Services Director

HANDLING AWKWARD CUSTOMERS
Letter 61: Denying a potential breach of contract

This is a tricky issue and one that would probably give the lawyers a field day. The legal issue is whether the prior contract set up with Mr Bone's predecessor overrides the contract which Mr Bone issued stating that "time was of the essence".

The legal issue aside, Michael Hardcastle clearly believes that he has a clear-cut case. The letter emphasises this belief, with phrases that are designed to knock his opponent off course: "I would like to draw your attention to the agreement..." and "...we deny your claim..." are examples. The only attempt to mollify Mr Bone occurs at the end, with the assurance that the order will be given priority.

IDENDEN INDUSTRIES
A division of Idenden Plc
Porter House, Hull HU7 4RF England

Tel 01482 119087 Fax 01482 119088
Registered in England No: 1218943

Jim Bone
Purchasing Manager
Wilson Smith Ltd
16 Willow Walk
Retford
Nottingham
NG6 8WS

12 February 1999

Dear Mr Bone

I am in receipt of your letter of 10 February.

You are claiming that if we do not deliver your goods ordered by 14 February that we shall be in breach of contract and you will cancel your order.

I would like to draw your attention to the agreement I set up with your predecessor, Malcolm Bute (see his letter dated 20 June 1997), which specifies that we shall only be in breach of contract if the goods are not supplied due to circumstances within our control. The industrial action at the distribution depot is clearly outside our control and we deny your claim to have the right to cancel the order.

We are doing everything in our power to compel our distributors to resolve the dispute swiftly. I am hopeful that the mediation being attempted will result in a speedy conclusion. I will ensure that your order is given priority, so that it is delivered to you at the earliest opportunity.

Yours sincerely

Michael Hardcastle
Sales Director

A situation in which orders are stopped because of non-payment is usually battled out between the two financial departments of the businesses. The sales and customer-services departments will become involved if there are orders pending.

Here, a friendly letter is sent mainly to inform the customer that payments are overdue. Both parties know it is not directly their responsibility but the appeal in the closing line: "Is there anything you can do?" is designed to influence the customer into taking action. The sender emphasises his own efficiency (contrasted with the customer's inefficiency) by saying that the next orders are ready to be despatched. A good, friendly, influential letter.

B & R HENDERSONS LTD

Marlows Road, Aberdeen AB20 5GT
Tel: 01224 267855 Fax: 01224 267977
Reg. No: 16497811 VAT No: 7387945

Helen Mitchell
Sales Manager
Good & Peabody
34 Kiln Street
Aberdeen
Scotland
AB8 7HY

13 August 1999

Dear Helen,

Re: Order Numbers 112568 and 112572

I am afraid that our Financial Director has put these orders on hold, due to payment problems. He faxed your office last week regarding the two overdue payments, but he has had no reply.

I have processed your orders, since I want them to be ready for despatch as soon as I am authorised to release them. However, this will not happen until the problem is resolved. Is there anything you can do?

I look forward to hearing from you.

Regards

Yours sincerly

Tina Cox
Sales Manager

REFUSING CUSTOMERS
Letter 63: Refusing to accept that a carriage charge be deducted

This letter is firm but friendly in tone. The main paragraph takes a persuasive stance with the phrase "...the carriage charge is only a contribution towards the final cost of delivering the goods to you". It is worth noting how the request to pay gradually builds up, rising to a crescendo in the final sentence. Criticism of the charge itself is deflected by an acknowledgement that it is only a contribution towards the cost. Next comes the point that the customer's prevarication over the delivery address contributed to the adjustment having to be made. The customer is subtly made to feel indebted to the supplier because "...we do everything we can to keep the charges as competitive as possible...", which phrase is designed to counteract the pain that is inflicted with the information that the supplier can't "...absorb the cost...". Note how the formal request to pay comes right at the end of the letter, in a firm sentence with a diplomatic double negative: "...I do not consider it unreasonable...", a softer, less abrasive way of saying 'please pay'.

GKT Products Ltd, Unit 10, Castleway Lane, Alloway, Ayr, KA7 4BE
Telephone (01292) 177900 Fax (01292) 199855   Reg. No: 17964583 VAT No: 679845

Mr B Holmes
Marketing Manager
Beresford-Biggs Ltd
39 Cavalry Drive
Histon
Cambs
CB7 4FE

16 June 1999

Dear Bill,

Our estimate no 229674 and our invoice no. 113975
Thank you for your letter of 12 June, concerning the carriage charge on our invoice.

The document on which we gave you our price was clearly headed as an estimate, and not a quotation as you claim. This permits us to make any necessary adjustments. The adjustment of the carriage charge is only a contribution towards the final cost of delivering the goods to you. You may also recall that you were unable to provide us with details of where the goods were to be delivered, when you asked us to give you a price. While we do everything we can to keep the charges for our goods as competitive as possible, I regret that on this occasion we are unable to absorb the cost of delivery in our prices.

Given all these circumstances, I do not consider it unreasonable to ask you to pay the carriage charge and would appreciate it if you could settle the account by the end of this month.

Yours sincerely

Tony Bright
Customer Services Manager

Occasionally a customer will want to change his order while it is being processed. If this involves additional cost, you should stand by the original order. "I am afraid it has not been possible..." lets the customer down lightly. Your aim, though, should be to appear as helpful as possible. Note how the supplier explains that he can do the extra copies and gives a provisional delivery date.

RPP Holdings Plc
35/38 New Road, Paignton, Devon TQ3 4UU
Tel: 01803 175653 Fax: 01803 187908
Reg. No: England 1976143

Mr A D Nelson
Sales Manager
Healthaware Co Ltd
56 Barrow Street
St Albans
Herts
AL2 1LD

14 October 1999

Dear Mr Nelson,

Your order no. 29785
Thank you for your fax, which I received this morning, asking if it was possible to increase your print order from 10,000 to 15,000 copies.

Your brochure went to press yesterday. I am afraid it has not been possible, therefore, for us to print an additional 5,000 copies within the existing run and give you the benefit of a lower price. We can still print the extra copies, although they will be at the slightly higher reprint price we gave you. We could deliver these by next Wednesday. Do you still want us to go ahead?

The main run, I am pleased to say, is going smoothly and we are on course to deliver it to you on Friday.

Yours sincerely

George Stevens
Account Manager

Some customers may try to abuse your terms and conditions. It can be tricky – do you risk losing a potential customer or allow yourself to be taken advantage of? The solution here is to take a firm line and point out politely how far your terms and conditions have been exceeded.

Note the technique designed to show how reasonable you are. The supplier achieves this by saying that he doesn't mind that one of his conditions has been exceeded; the real objection is to the condition in which the shirt has been returned.

H J KINGSLEY (NORWICH) LTD

Kingsley House, Morris Street, Norwich NR6 7JM
Tel: (01603) 117097 Fax: (01603) 117099 Reg. No: England 12086215 VAT No: 8793519

Mr Lester Patterson
30 Virgin Close
Doncaster
S Yorks
DN9 0DB

26 May 1999

Dear Mr Patterson,

I am writing concerning your request for a refund on the shirt which you purchased from us.

As you know, under our conditions of sale, we offer all our customers a ten-day, no-quibble, money-back guarantee, provided the goods are returned within this period in a saleable condition.

We despatched your parcel to you on 15 March. The parcel in which you returned the item to us was date stamped 16 May. Even allowing five days for our parcel to reach you, this means that you have had the goods in your possession for 56 days, some 41 days outside our guarantee period. While we would be willing to overlook this point, we were concerned to find that the shirt you returned had clearly been worn and was soiled to an extent that it cannot be offered for resale.

I very much regret, therefore, that we shall be unable to offer you a refund. I am returning the shirt to you under separate cover.

Yours sincerely

P Phillips
Customer Services Manager

Customers' letters of thanks are some of the best (although often the rarest) letters to receive in business. When they do come, you should not ignore them. Instead, you should respond, reaffirming in the customer's mind that you are a good company to be doing business with.

The style of this letter is good because it takes a modest approach by saying "...we haven't done anything 'special'...". The closing line has a nice ring to it, showing the real appreciation that is felt for the letter. The customer cannot fail to think this is a business worth dealing with.

Grange & Turner Ltd

32 WESTBOURN ROAD, WITNEY, OXON OX6 7HY

Telephone (01993) 107888
Fax (01993) 107843

Reg. No: England 13078453
VAT No: 75698764

Ms Olive Short
Purchasing Manager
Parker Bright Ltd
72 Dudley Road
Brighton
Essex
BR6 5RT

13 March 1999

Dear Ms Short

Thank you for your letter of 7th March, which reached me today.

It was very kind of you to take the trouble to write to say how our service has helped you. As I am sure you are aware it is always very uplifting to be thanked - and I find letters of thanks when we haven't done anything 'special', just gone about providing our normal service, the most pleasant of all.

How do we seem to match your needs?

Firstly, there is quite a lot of choice. Approximately 30 new products are introduced each month, roughly one hundred different products in the course of a year. So there is good chance of meeting the need of the moment of each individual person.

But secondly, and much more importantly, it is the market that ultimately selects the products. It is the products that sell well (and are not returned under our guarantee) that stay in the leaflets. In fact, they have been voted for by other customers. The needs of one customer are often very like the need of another.

So we don't need a mole in your business – we just have to watch what everyone else wants! Of course, we make the initial choice, but even this is based on years of experience of what it is that makes a bestselling product that everybody wants to buy.

Once again, thank you very much indeed for taking the trouble to write to me.

Yours sincerely

Herbert Short
Manager

THANKING CUSTOMERS
Letter 67: Thank-you letter for hospitality

When writing letters of thanks, it is always nice if you thank, not just the person you are writing to, but also to ask for your thanks to be passed on to other people you met.

Saying something appreciative which engenders a positive feeling, for example, how your expectations were exceeded, is another useful tip for earning credit with the customer. This is done here with the declaration that the company is ahead of the game in fields other than 'systems'.

Charles Cunningham Ltd

29 Baker Street, LONDON N34 6GH England
Tel: (0171) 015 1290 Fax: (0171) 015 1271
Reg. No: England 1104398135 VAT No: 82108643

Ms Debra Clifton
Vice President
Winger & Ewing Inc.
7853 Wateridge Drive
Pleasanton
CA 95488
USA

24 May 1999

Dear Deb,

Having arrived safely back in the UK and having adjusted to the time difference, the size of the place and the fact that coffee is served at the end of meals, I am now in a position to write to you concerning our visit to your offices.

Firstly, I would like to say thank you to you and all your colleagues for the wonderful hospitality and the time you were willing to devote to our visit. We would be grateful if you would thank your colleagues on our behalf.

We were very impressed with the obvious professionalism that runs throughout your organisation. Having been told that you were "the number one for systems"; not only was this confirmed but, our impression is, that you are excellent at all the other aspects as well.

All this leaves to say is thank you once again for your hospitality; I hope we will have the opportunity to respond in a similar fashion if you, or any of your colleagues, visit the UK.

With kind regards,

Yours sincerely,

D. Dean
Director

This letter shows how, even though the sender, Thomas Griffiths, doesn't know Mr Drake, a friendly, informal tone can be struck. It is even better, because the customer, who had vowed (in an earlier letter) never to have anything more to do with the business after a hiccup in the customer-service system, was won back by a highly personalised letter explaining what went wrong.

Asking the reader to imagine how encouraging it is to receive this type of letter has the effect of pulling the customer closer – getting him to empathise with your situation – and build the common bond you have.

The enthusiasm shines through in the use of adjectives designed to emphasise the genuine feeling of pleasure:"...your extremely pleasant letter...";
"...very considerably...";
"...even greater pleasure...",
which all add up to a great sense of warmth.

Grange & Turner Ltd

32 WESTBOURN ROAD, WITNEY, OXON OX6 7HY

Telephone (01993) 107888
Fax (01993) 107843

Reg. No: England 13078453
VAT No: 75698764

Mr D Drake
24 Berry Green
Wellingborough
Northants
NN43 5MN

12 August 1999

Dear Mr Drake

Thank you very much indeed for your extremely pleasant letter, which arrived this morning. It brightened my day very considerably.

I do not know whether you can imagine how very encouraging it is in a mail-order company to get letters of appreciation (most people are moved to write only to complain!). And of course there is even greater pleasure in restoring a damaged relationship with a long-standing customer.

Thank you very much indeed for taking the trouble to write to reassure me. Please do let me know if anything goes wrong again.

Yours sincerely

Thomas Griffiths
Director

THANKING CUSTOMERS
Letter 69: Thanking a good client, slightly cheekily

If you decide to write an informal, jovial letter, make sure it doesn't overstep the mark. The person receiving this letter would need to be on very good terms with the sender.

In playing on the list of excuses that could have been made, there is a danger that the tone could be misconstrued and interpreted as being heavily sarcastic. The letter redeems itself, though, with the genuine note of thanks at the end.

Note how, even though the main paragraph has been written as a list, it is left as a piece of consecutive prose, which reflects how it would have been spoken. The numbers are there to emphasise, rather than separate, the text.

Fenner & Sons

16 George Street, Woodbridge,
Suffolk IP3 7KL
Tel: (01394) 198423
Fax: (01394) 198444
Registered in England: 91221299
VAT No: 919129075 80

Mr Bob Holmes
Senior Buyer
H J Kingsley (Norwich) Ltd
Kingsley House
Morris Street
Norwich
NR6 7JM

13 September 1999

Dear Bob

Just a note to say thank you for the cheque.

And how wonderfully refreshing, to receive a cheque the day after being told it is being sent!

Thank you for not: 1) passing the cheque on to a colleague on holiday for counter-signature, 2) despatching it to your Kings Lynn accounting centre for final approval and speedy processing, 3) including it in the next cheque run, 4) endeavouring to ensure it receives priority attention even though (a) Tuesday is too late in the week to be included in this week's cheque run, and (b) payments due after the 5th cannot normally be actioned in the same month.

In other words, hearty thanks.

Kind regards

John Smith
Accounts Manager

If you end up getting business (or even the prospect of business) from a recommendation, it is not only courteous but also sound business sense to thank the person who recommended you. If you don't thank them, why should they bother to do it again? People like to feel appreciated and useful; it will make your associate more inclined to recommend you again in future. Ignoring the person who made the recommendation looks as if you are taking him for granted. Alternatively, he may think you didn't like the potential client and next time an opportunity comes along he will send it to a competitor!

RPP Holdings Plc
35/38 New Road, Paignton, Devon TQ3 4UU
Tel: 01803 175653 Fax: 01803 187908
Reg. No: England 1976143

Mr David Cross
Sales Director
P P Plus Ltd
Grove Industrial Estate
Warwick
CV7 1PL

19 February 1999

Dear David

I am writing to thank you for recommending me to Peter Norman at DAS UK. Your kindness is very much appreciated.

If I remember rightly, you did, in fact, recommend me to this firm when they had offices in Kingston, although at the time nothing came of the enquiry.

We have put a price to them on a job of printing 4-colour process posters and, if anything comes of it, I will be in touch with you.

I hope that you are keeping well and busy; things are still very quiet here. We keep getting a lot of enquiries but many fall by the wayside when followed up. Anyway, we have survived two major recessions so we must be doing something right, and things are bound to pick up eventually.

I remember the last time I spoke to you that things were quiet at your end also; I hope things are now going better for you now.

Thank you once again for your kindness.

Yours sincerely

Richard Price
Director

If there is a gap between appointments, customers or suppliers may feel that their interests are not being looked after or they may notice a slip in service caused by the change-over. To prevent this happening it is worth announcing details of the new appointment and the date when the new person is due to join, in a personal letter. Emphasising how much experience they have gives confidence in the competence of the person. Offering a back-up or intermediate contact is also a good idea, in case an urgent matter arises before the appointee arrives.

Thomas King & Palmer Ltd
serving the world

24 Fuller Road, Welling,
Kent DA16 7JP
Tel : (01322) 100132
Fax : (01322) 100178

Reg. No : England 1212298762
VAT No : 92905643

Mr D Jenkins
Director
Chester Wood Ltd
35 Grand Hill Road
Waverton
Chester
CH6 5FG

30 August 1999

Dear Mr Jenkins,

New General Manager

We are pleased to announce the appointment of Gerald Best as General Manager from September 6th 1999. His appointment follows the retirement, due to ill health, of Tony March, in August.

Gerald comes to us with considerable experience of marketing and he will be contacting all of our clients as soon as he arrives, to introduce himself and to deal with any queries which may arise.

We are happy to assure all of our clients of the same, continuing, high-quality service for which we are proud to enjoy such a good reputation.

Should you, however, have any urgent enquiries, please do not hesitate to contact me personally.

Yours sincerely

Brian Moore
Director

This is one of those 'just keeping in touch' letters that is not absolutely necessary but is often welcomed by the recipient.

It can be quite a shock to 'phone a company, only to be told that the person you wish to speak to has left. Letters like this also benefit customers and suppliers, because they are kept informed about who to contact. If a new contact-name is not given, the customer may feel that your company isn't concerned to communicate with him, so why should he keep doing business with you, even though such claims may be totally unjustified.

If a lot of the goodwill in the relationship is tied up in the personal nature of the contact, it is worth bringing into the letter a comment expressing your confidence in the continuing relationship after you have left.

Wright & Simpson

157 Colder Way
Basingstoke
Hants RG21 5TG
Tel: (01256) 125907
Fax: (01256) 190986

Mr Robin Gillett
Marketing Director
Taylor Jones Ltd
23 Green St
Liverpool
L17 6HY

28 July 1999

Dear Robin,

Just a quick note to let you know that I have successfully completed my assignment at Wright and Simpson and will be taking up my new position as Director of International Business with Jackson Powell on 10th August.

I believe that Wright and Simpson has once again regained its position as one of the leading training consultancies and I am pleased to have been associated with this success.

It is also my pleasure to advise you that the General Manager's position will be filled in-house by Graham Fox; and he will be assisted by John Birch and Sheila Cox, who will be responsible for enquiries and order-processing respectively.

It has been a pleasure working with you and I am confident you will continue to enjoy a long and successful association with Wright and Simpson.

Best regards

Yours sincerely

Stuart Davis
Consultant

Partners: EG Wright MA & FA Simpson

KEEPING CUSTOMERS INFORMED
Letter 73: Reawakening a business relationship

You may run into an old acquaintance with whom you used to do business. You would like to reawaken that business relationship. This letter attempts to bridge the gap, with a copy of the latest catalogue.

Note how the writer draws the reader's attention to the content of the catalogue, not just the fact there is a catalogue. This device tries to tempt the reader to turn the page – and to stop them from putting the catalogue to one side.

H J KINGSLEY (NORWICH) LTD
Kingsley House, Morris Street, Norwich NR6 7JM
Tel: (01603) 117097 Fax: (01603) 117099 Reg. No: England 12086215 VAT No: 8793519

Ms Gail Wilson
Marketing Manager
Bridgewater Bright Ltd
76 Chalmers Way
Andover
Hants
SP4 7JK

28 September 1999

Dear Gail,

In conversation with your colleague Mary yesterday, it emerged that you have not had up-to-date information from us recently on our range of products. So I am putting that right immediately.

As promised, I am enclosing our newly revised catalogue, which brings you right up to date with our new products and innovations.

At the front of the catalogue are the most recent acquisitions, with a breakdown of their key features. The bestsellers follow and I am certain these will be familiar to you. At the back, we have more specialist topics, some of which are esoteric enough for the most confirmed devotees. I hope these will be of interest to you.

If you would like further information, please ring us on (01603) 117097 or fax us on (01603) 117099.

Best wishes,

Yours sincerely

Nina Davis
Marketing Manager

Gaining feedback from customers is essential. How else are you going to improve your service? Feedback from questionnaires can also provide some wonderful surprises – have you ever thought about using the favourable feedback as testimonials on future promotions? There is no more powerful seller of a product or service than a satisfied customer.

One difficulty with customer-attitude surveys is the comparatively low response they generate. A small, low-cost gift acts as an incentive and may increase the number of responses that you receive.

Grange & Turner Ltd

32 WESTBOURN ROAD, WITNEY, OXON OX6 7HY

Telephone (01993) 107888
Fax (01993) 107843

Reg. No: England 13078453
VAT No: 75698764

Mr F V Bland
Director
Taylor, Taylor & Hall
25 Glebe Lane
Darlington
Co Durham
DL6 5TG

16 June 1999

Dear Mr Bland

As a company committed to providing a quality service, we like to keep in regular touch with your needs and your views of the products we produce and promote.

To maintain our high standard of quality products and service to you, I would be very grateful if you could complete the enclosed questionnaire.

In appreciation of your time, I shall be delighted to send you one of our superb quality Parker Pens on receipt of your completed questionnaire.

I look forward to receiving your reply and hope that we continue to be helpful to you in the future.

Yours sincerely

Mrs A Frank
Marketing Director

If you find customers buying once from you but not again, it can be worthwhile conducting a customer-service exercise to find out why they are not coming back to you. This letter dresses the investigation up to make it look like an after-sales service questionnaire. If you are asking for a large chunk of time, it may be worth sending a personalised letter in advance, explaining what you want to do and why.

Note how the letter empathises with the customer: "I appreciate this is a busy time for you..." and rather than asking her to 'phone you, announces that you will be in touch in a day or two. If you do say this, make sure not to leave it too long, so that the customer doesn't forget your letter.

H J KINGSLEY (NORWICH) LTD
Kingsley House, Morris Street, Norwich NR6 7JM
Tel: (01603) 117097 Fax: (01603) 117099 Reg. No: England 12086215 VAT No: 8793519

Ms Ruth Hope
Senior Buyer
Frank Fuller Ltd
34 Crester Street
Windrush
Oxon
OX7 9JU

2 October 1999

Dear Ruth,

I hope the last order we supplied to you was satisfactory and met your expectations.

We are currently looking at ways of improving our product range and services to our customers. I appreciate this is a busy time for you but I wonder if you would be prepared to spend half an hour discussing the service that you have received from us; what your expectations are about the products we supply; how those expectations have been met or exceeded and where you feel there is room for improvement. I would like to cover everything from initial supply of the order to the after-sales service that you have received.

I hope you are willing to help us in this matter. If I may, I will telephone you in a day or so to fix up a convenient date for us to meet.

Yours sincerely

Nina Davis
Marketing Manager

Debt collection and credit control

3

Chapter 3

Debt collection and credit control

Chasing for payment can be a soul-destroying activity, as customers either try to wriggle out of paying at all, or test your patience by seeing how long they can go without having to pay up. Many of the letters in this chapter are proven winners at getting recalcitrant customers to dig deep into their pockets and pay their dues. So you can be confident about using them, knowing that they have been genuinely tried and tested.

Choosing the right tone

Hitting the right note, first time, in a letter demanding payment, is not always easy. To help you choose, the collection letters have been divided broadly into three areas, as the Contents show: straightforward first-time demands for payment (letters 76–79); stronger demands (letters 80–83) and final demands that choose sterner phrases (letters 84–87).

Incentives and deterrents

If you want to try to avoid sending a letter chasing payment, the section on granting credit (letters 88–91) shows how to open a new account, how to notify a new account of their terms of trading, how to offer an incentive for prompt payment and announce a credit surcharge.

Queries and disputes

Sorting these out need not always be a headache. Letters 97 and 98 show how to handle them successfully.

Handling a demand for payment

If you find yourself on the receiving end of a demand for payment, letters 99 and 100 shows how to keep the pack at bay for a little longer.

DEMANDS FOR PAYMENT
Letter 76: Gently reminding a customer about payment not received

The tone of this collection letter is neutral. It is a simple enquiry, taking a non-confrontational standpoint.

Enquiring if there is a problem with the order is a subtle attempt to flush out any reasons for non-payment. Accounts departments are often the last to hear about any reasons why an invoice has not been paid. Note the fairly emphatic last sentence, not just asking when the invoice will be paid but for "...*immediate* settlement".

 RPP Holdings Plc
35/38 New Road, Paignton, Devon TQ3 4UU
Tel: 01803 175653 Fax: 01803 187908
Reg. No. England 1976143

FAX MESSAGE TO: Janet Turner

FAX No: 015594 887766

FROM: Sue Frost - Accounts   DATE: 17 May 1999

OUR INVOICE NO. 115689 DATED 11.02.99
Our invoice no. 115689 dated 11.02.99, which refers to your order no. AL2158, should have been paid at the very latest by the end of April.

To date, we have not received your payment. I wonder if there has been a problem with this order of which we are not aware?

If not, please arrange immediate settlement.

Many thanks

Sue Frost

THIS MESSAGE CONSISTS OF ONE PAGE. PLEASE LET ME KNOW BY PHONE OR FAX IMMEDIATELY IF ANY PAGE IS ILLEGIBLE.

DEMANDS FOR PAYMENT
Letter 77: Requesting confirmation of when items will be paid for

This is an initial letter chasing payment. Its sole purpose is to exact confirmation of when payments will be forthcoming. Note how the tone is completely neutral and unhostile. Laying out the outstanding items in a table, giving relevant dates, invoice references, details of what was purchased and the value of each invoice, will help prevent the company from claiming that they can't find the information.

RPP Holdings Plc
35/38 New Road, Paignton, Devon TQ3 4UU
Tel: 01803 175653 Fax: 01803 187908
Reg. No: England 1976143

Fax Message to:	Maurice Brown Manilla Stationery Ltd
Fax Number:	0171 189 2008
From:	Tom Richards, Financial Director
Date:	31st July 1999

Listed below are open items on your account that I believe are past their due date for payment. Please confirm when each will be paid.

Manilla Stationery Ltd - Sales Account History

Tp	Date	Ref	Details	Amount
SI	03.03.99	20331	M/R continuous computer paper	£214.73
SI	10.03.99	20334	DL envelopes Non-window S/S	£522.00
SI	03.04.99	20354	M/R continuous computer paper	£864.23
SI	21.04.99	20362	A4 Photocopier paper	£442.00

Total due:	**£2042.96**

Regards

Tom Richards
Finance Director

THIS MESSAGE CONSISTS OF 1 PAGE. PLEASE LET US KNOW BY PHONE OR FAX IMMEDIATELY IF ANY PAGE IS ILLEGIBLE.

DEMANDS FOR PAYMENT
Letter 78: Reminding a customer about credit terms and requesting payment

With new trading partners, you can never tell what the payment record is going to be like. This one adopts a rather prickly tone. The line at the end of the first sentence: "I look after the money at Simpson & Martin" is designed to emphasise that this is not a standard chasing letter but about a more serious issue. The prickly feeling is enhanced in the second paragraph, with the metaphor: "...this thorny issue of payment...".

The organised way in which the Finance Director knows exactly which payments are meant to be made at what time contrasts with the chaotic payment received, suggesting that the customer's is not in order. The goal here is to make it quite clear to the the trading partner that you are aware of what is going on and so encourage them into a more timely payment pattern, before alternative action becomes imperative.

SIMPSON
& MARTIN

39 TOP STREET
STOKE-ON-TRENT
ST2 3DR UNITED KINGDOM
Tel: (01782) 156232 Fax: (01782) 120899
Reg. No: England 96223978 VAT No: 91210674

Mr Frank Little
Finance Director
P G Black Ltd
Turner Way
Denton
Peterborough
PE6 8HJ

26 May 1999

Dear Mr Little,

Thank you for the business which you have brought to us; we've invoiced you almost £10,786.56 since the beginning of our financial year (August). We haven't met, but I look after the money at Simpson & Martin.

It's always pleasing to see new business - but even more pleasing to be paid for that business. And it is this thorny issue of payment that causes me to write to you.

Four orders have been accepted on "Mailing Date plus 60 days" credit and subsequent orders have been accepted on "Mailing Date plus 30 days" credit. This means that we expect to receive payment within, respectively, 60 and 30 days of the mailing date. But this has, so far, not happened.

We expected to receive a payment at the end of March for your orders 115684 and 115712 (see attached account history). And we expected two further payments to follow.

We did finally receive a payment on 12 May. But we have had no advice from your accounts to say which invoices are being paid or what the gross amount transmitted was, and the amount received does not tally with any combination of outstanding invoices.

In the interim, more invoices have fallen due for payment. Please confirm to me that these will be paid promptly and that future business will be conducted as expected.

I look forward to hearing from you.

Yours sincerely

William Patterson
Finance Director

New arrangements that require a special payment – for example, a commission as in this case – can be easy to forget, particularly if it is due only once a year. A reminder is almost certainly necessary.

Where the amount owing is a percentage of a larger sum, don't forget to list each contract, calculate the total, and show how the percentage was arrived at. If the company here had simply issued an invoice for £9,699.72, there would have been no way of telling how that sum had accrued.

Tyler & Piper Associates

76 Whites Lane, Stevenage, Herts SG1 8JP England
Tel: (01438) 186465 Fax: (01438) 164323

Mr P Street
International Sales Manager
Hughes & Hickle Ltd
5 Bedford Way
Milton Keynes
MK55 6JJ

23 September 1999

Dear Mr Street

Commission Invoice No: 119747

I would like to remind you of our Export Consultation Agreement and draw your attention to the clients below who placed orders in 1998. A 10% commission is now outstanding.

Holz Engineering (Germany)	£32,047.05
Pierres (France)	£21,106.17
Jolon Export/Import Co. (Burma)	£43,844.00
TOTAL	£96,997.22
Total Commission due @ 10%	£ 9,699.72

We are, therefore, looking forward to the receipt of your cheque for the above sum by return.

Yours sincerely,

John Dunn
Financial Manager

Partners: DA Tyler BA & SR Piper MA

STRONGER DEMANDS FOR PAYMENT
Letter 80: Notifying that an account is overdue and requesting payment

This chaser is a fairly pleasant example of a final demand. Referring to the series of chasing faxes and telephone call acts as a reminder of how much effort you have exerted, without response.

Note how the amount outstanding and account number are outside the main body of the text, the implication being that everyone knows what is outstanding.

Giving the bank details again will pre-empt any excuses that this information is missing. The phrase at the end of the fax "...in view of the one-sided nature of our correspondence..." adds a touch of mordant wit that should increase the embarrassment of the recipient as well as slightly drawing the sting of the serious threat to begin legal action against him.

Thomas King & Palmer Ltd
serving the world

24 Fuller Road, Welling,
Kent DA16 7JP
Tel : (01322) 100132
Fax : (01322) 100178

Reg. No : England 1212298762
VAT No : 92905643

Facsimile Cover Sheet

To: Peter Johnson
Company: Peter Johnson Inc.
Phone: 00 1 505 171 623
Fax: 00 1 505 171 698

From: James Steven
Company: Thomas King & Palmer
Phone: 01322 100132
Fax: 01322 100178

Date: 7 November 1999
No of Pages: 1

Please let us know by phone or fax immediately if any page is missing or has been garbled in transmission.

Amount outstanding: £2658.89   Account number: PL98358

I have now sent you a number of fax messages and spoken personally to you on the telephone (on 1 October).

My most recent fax was sent on 25 October. I am disappointed to have had no response to it.

Please will you arrange immediate payment of the amount due to our bankers:-

RSH Bank,
Main Street, Welling (Sort Code 10-12-13)
For account of: Thomas King & Palmer, Account No.3
Account number: 26479310

If we have not received payment within seven days then, in view of the   one-sided nature of our correspondence, I can see no option but to seek the assistance of attorneys to resolve the situation.

Yours sincerely

James Steven
Financial Manager

This letter strikes a polite tone, although it contains a veiled threat. The seriousness is conveyed by stating that the letter has been sent by recorded delivery (to nullify any excuse that it was not received and must have been 'lost in the post').

Signing the letter 'Legal Department' (even though the signatory may not be a lawyer) is designed to apply further pressure.

It is clear that legal action will be taken, but note how this is not made explicit, only implied in the euphemism "...passed into other hands...". Another effective phrase that can be applied in similar letters is "...render this action unnecessary...".

Charles Cunningham Ltd

29 Baker Street, LONDON N34 6GH England
Tel: (0171) 015 1290 Fax: (0171) 015 1271
Reg. No: England 1104398135 VAT No: 82108643

<u>By Recorded Delivery</u>

Hugh Buggs
Financial Director
Edwards & Davis Ltd
Western HouseBridge Street
Preston
Lancs
PR5 3FD

19 May 1999

Dear Mr Buggs,

I am surprised to have received no reply to our previous letter, asking for immediate settlement of the attached statement, which is long overdue.

Unfortunately, I cannot allow this account to remain unpaid any longer, and I regret that the matter will be passed into other hands in seven days.

I am still hopeful that you will render this action unnecessary by sending your remittance in full to arrive here within seven days.

Yours sincerely,

Keith Vail
Legal Department

STRONGER DEMANDS FOR PAYMENT
Letter 82: Requesting more timely payment

Quoting the words of the debtor back at him is a valuable technique for inducing payment. The person is made to feel that he is not to be trusted, having broken his promises.

Note some of the emphatic phrases that intensify the meaning behind a sentence: "I must say..."; "...I do not see why..."; "...have still to hear..."; I would like at the very least...". All these strengthen the thrust of the letter.

Wright & Simpson

157 Colder Way
Basingstoke
Hants RG21 5TG
Tel: (01256) 125907
Fax: (01256) 190986

Eric Barker
Director
Charles Cunningham Ltd
29 Baker Street
London
N34 6GH

9 March 1999

Dear Mr Barker

Thank you for your fax, regarding payment for your orders.

Our bank details are:

National Westminster Bank
Acc No: 46789124   Sort Code: 00 12 34

I must say that I regard your statement that we should "expect payment in approximately two weeks" as extremely disappointing.

Outstanding Amount: £768.54   Invoice Nos: 316789 & 316790

The above invoices are dated 23 January and on our 30-day terms were due for payment by 28 February. As these payments are already overdue, I do not see why we should tolerate a further two weeks' delay; we have still to hear when one of the invoices might be paid at all.

I would like, at the very least, a firm commitment for the latest date we can expect payment – preferably well within the two weeks.

I look forward to hearing from you.

Yours sincerely

Mary Taylor
Customer Account Manager

P.S. We supplied our bank details as you requested in January "in order that payment for the above invoices could be made as soon as possible".

Partners: EG Wright MA & FA Simpson

Threats are omitted from this letter but the message is just as potent. The customer's sense of fair play and common courtesy is called into question, by the perfectly reasonable request that 'we are only trying to talk to you'.

The last sentence should strike a chord – the implication being that a failure to pay will mean your services being withdrawn. The 'wall of silence' idea is echoed in the request for a 'communicative' business relationship in the final sentence.

H J KINGSLEY (NORWICH) LTD

Kingsley House, Morris Street, Norwich NR6 7JM
Tel: (01603) 117097 Fax: (01603) 117099 Reg. No: England 12086215 VAT No: 8793519

FAX MESSAGE TO: Jim Clements Copy to Accounts Dept

FAX No: 01654 789654

FROM : Tim Good, Financial Director DATE: 6 July 1999

THIS MESSAGE CONSISTS OF ONE PAGE. PLEASE LET ME KNOW BY PHONE OR FAX IMMEDIATELY IF ANY PAGE IS ILLEGIBLE.

Our Invoice No. SP56732
In April this year you ordered, a shrink-wrapping machine from us: Order No 115682, placed by Jim Clements.

Payment on our invoice (no. SP56732, copy follows) for this order was due 30 days from invoice date - i.e. 31 May 1999.

I have sent faxes to both yourself and to your accounts department, asking for confirmation that the invoice has been received and that it will be paid. It is now several months overdue.

To date I have had no reply.

We supply to valued customers in good faith and on the understanding that what we supply will be paid for. It is somewhat disconcerting when we endeavour to communicate with a customer regarding payment and are met with a wall of silence.

Please arrange for immediate payment direct to our bankers:
RSH Bank Plc – England
Sort Code: 00 12 34
Account Name: HJ Kingsley (Norwich) Ltd
Account No: 978164978

I look forward to receiving confirmation of payment and to a long, fruitful and communicative business relationship.

Yours sincerely

Tim Good
Finance Director

FINAL DEMANDS FOR PAYMENT
Letter 84: Notifying that an account is seriously overdue

This is a stern but, on the whole, polite letter. It gives the recipient an opportunity to give a reason why payment is being withheld. It is interesting because the other hands into which this case will be put, if payment is not received, are "collection agents", which somehow has a slightly more sinister tone than lawyers. It conjures up images of the men in dark coats being sent round to sort things out. Another interesting feature is the closing line. This phrase "...please disregard this letter..." is usually found in correspondence with consumers (rather than other businesses) but it is useful if you don't want to appear more heavy-handed than is absolutely necessary.

B & R HENDERSONS LTD
Marlows Road, Aberdeen AB20 5GT
Tel: 01224 267855 Fax: 01224 267977
Reg. No: 16497811 VAT No: 7387945

Mr A Scott
General Manager
Scott Bros
Morton House
Station Road
Glasgow
G6 7HY

13 September 1999

Dear Mr Scott

Account No: 527BSGPR
Post Date: 10.07.99
Outstanding amount: £21.86

Your account with us is now SERIOUSLY OVERDUE. Should you have any justification for withholding payment, we would be obliged to hear from you concerning the problem.

However, if we do not hear from you by return or receive payment for the above account within the next seven days, you will leave us no alternative but to instruct our Collection Agents to take sufficient action to secure the amount outstanding.

We would very much regret having to take this decision and suggest that you immediately make the necessary arrangement for payment.

If you have sent your remittance in the last few days, please disregard this letter.

Yours sincerely,

Jane Fuller
Credit Controller

'We've been rumbled' would be the response of the recipient of this letter (if the business was in genuine trouble). If the suspicion of insolvency is unfounded on the other hand, it should provoke a firm rebuttal – no genuine business likes to get this kind of reputation because it is going to dent its credit rating severely.

An interesting point worth noting is the use of a specific time and day for payment to be received. If the writer had put "...received payment by Tuesday 21 November...", the creditor would not be able to take action until first thing Wednesday. Putting a specific time limit means that appropriate action can be taken at one minute past noon on the Tuesday. A small point, but one worth remembering if you are very anxious to get your money back. Setting a time limit also makes you sound more determined – as if your lawyers are lined up, ready and waiting to be sent in.

Charles Cunningham Ltd

29 Baker Street, LONDON N34 6GH England
Tel: (0171) 015 1290 Fax: (0171) 015 1271
Reg. No: England 1104398135 VAT No: 82108643

Mr E Wright
Senior Partner
Wright & Simpson
157 Colder Way
Basingstoke
Hants
RG6 5TG

12 November 1999

Dear Mr Wright,

Our Undisputed Invoice No. 005694
Your account has been passed to me for attention, because we are receiving from your business the classic signals of one about to go under. Apparently, our phone messages are not responded to, and the only member of your staff we can speak to is a temp, who is unable to provide any answers.

I sincerely hope that this is not the case, and that there is some misunderstanding which can be easily explained.

But we are owed £3652.00 for our undisputed invoice no. 005694, relating to your order no. BNN5643. And payment was due at the end of September.

To avoid any further misunderstanding, please forward your payment by return.

Please treat this as a formal and final request. If we have not received payment by noon on Tuesday 21 November, legal proceedings will commence without further notice to you.

Yours sincerely,

Keith Vail
Legal Department

FINAL DEMANDS FOR PAYMENT
Letter 86: Asking for payment in full – keeping up the pressure

Some customers may try to buy time to pay off their debts. They may have genuine difficulties that can be solved in time and a more conciliatory approach may be appropriate.

But if they have not provided you with a satisfactory reason for the delay and you suspect that they are simply playing for time, this type of letter may be necessary. It contains some good phrases: "We appreciate this act of good faith..." and "...regrettably, this amount does not clear your account...".

RPP Holdings Plc
35/38 New Road, Paignton, Devon TQ3 4UU
Tel: 01803 175653 Fax: 01803 187908
Reg. No: England 1976143

Mrs Jane Markham
Finance Director
Grange & Turner Ltd
32 Westbourn Road
Witney
Oxon
OX6 7HY

27 February 1999

Dear Mrs Markham

Re. Outstanding account
Thank you for your cheque for £1500 in partial settlement of your account.

We appreciate this act of good faith but, regrettably, this amount does not clear your account and leaves £1297.98 still outstanding on invoices that are now 76 days overdue for payment.

We shall give you seven days from the date of this letter to settle your account. If we have not received payment in full by that date, we shall instigate court proceedings to recover the sum.

Yours sincerely

Tom Richards
Finance Director

FINAL DEMANDS FOR PAYMENT
Letter 87: Announcing court proceedings in seven days

If you send this type of letter you must be certain about carrying out your threat. Some unscrupulous companies may decide to call your bluff and test your threat before deciding to settle.

This letter has got past the threatening stage. Its power lies in the double implication that they will not only take you to court to recover the sum but also consider winding up your company.

GKT Products Ltd, Unit 10, Castleway Lane, Alloway, Ayr, KA7 4BE
Telephone (01292) 177900 Fax (01292) 199855   Reg. No: 17964583 VAT No: 679845

Mr T Freeborn
Managing Director
F & G (Packaging) Ltd
12 The Industrial Park
Morley Road
Dartford
Kent
DA1 2TH

12 November 1999

Dear Mr Freeborn

Account Number: 2698745
Amount Due: £4896.89

This account has now been passed into legal hands. We will issue Court proceedings against you seven days from the date of this letter, unless before then we receive a cheque for this sum.

There will be no further warning. The proceedings will include additional claims for legal costs and statutory interest resulting from your prior failure to pay. Upon judgment we will forthwith execute against you.

If we are not placed in full funds within the above time limit, we reserve the right alternatively, where grounds exist, to instruct our Solicitors to issue the relevant petition under the Insolvency Act 1986.

We look forward to your immediate remittance.

Yours sincerely

For & on behalf of
GKT Products Ltd
<u>Legal Department</u>

This letter starts an account on a firm, business-like basis. Four key points are worth noting and including in similar letters: an opportunity for the account holder to correct any errors in the address details; their attention drawn to the terms and conditions of sale and their point of contact in the sales department named. The most important piece of information, the credit limit and terms, is given prominence in the heart of the letter. Note that the word 'concurrent' is used here, to prevent the other party from running up invoices that exceed £1500 until it has paid the amount due within the 30-day period.

H J KINGSLEY (NORWICH) LTD
Kingsley House, Morris Street, Norwich NR6 7JM
Tel: (01603) 117097 Fax: (01603) 117099 Reg. No: England 12086215 VAT No: 8793519

Mr L Evans
Purchasing Manager
Parker Glass Ltd
Unit 27 Willow Park
Christchurch
Dorset
BH23 6MM

27 April 1999

Dear Mr Evans

Thank you for your application for a credit account. We have pleasure informing you that your account is now open; your account number is 013649780.

Please check the above address details and inform us of any amendments.

A credit limit of £1500 has been fixed to your account, concurrent to our 30 days net credit terms. Subject to your payments reaching us on the said date and your adherence to our terms, we will review your credit status on application.

If you have any queries regarding our conditions of sale, they can be found on the reverse of most of our documentation. Additionally, our accounts department will be more than pleased to advise you.

Your Area Sales Manager, Mr Thomas Carter, has been informed that your account is now open.

Yours sincerely

Rose Adams
Accounts Administrator

When a new account is opened, the terms of trading should have been agreed in advance.

Before accepting an order on a credit basis, the company should take up trade references and conduct a credit check, to ensure there is a good prospect of receiving payment. The company should then confirm that a credit account has been opened, as in the letter here.

This is a good opportunity to inform the customer about individual operating procedures, which will lead to a harmonious business relationship and reduce the chance of nasty surprises being sprung.

B & R HENDERSONS LTD

Marlows Road, Aberdeen AB20 5GT
Tel: 01224 267855 Fax: 01224 267977
Reg. No: 16497811 VAT No: 7387945

Helen Mitchell
Sales Manager
Good & Peabody
34 Kiln Street
Aberdeen
Scotland
AB8 7HY

13 August 1999

Dear Ms Mitchell

Thank you for returning our credit application form.

I have pleasure in informing you that a credit-trading account has been opened for you, with a limit of £3000 as requested. For your information, here are a few important points concerning our operating procedures:

1. Office hours are 8.30am to 5.30pm inclusive, Monday to Friday.

2. Orders are dispatched by carrier on a three-working-day service. This means that for orders received by, for example, 12 noon on Monday, delivery will be on Thursday.

   2.1 Next-day delivery is available, at an extra cost.

3. A detailed, but un-priced, delivery note is included in each consignment.

4. Invoices are posted at the time of dispatch and often arrive ahead of the goods.

5. Your sales contact is either Sue Spreadborough or Richard Selby but, for your convenience, all of our staff can accept telephone orders.

6. The threshold for carriage-paid orders is £500, although we have no minimum order quantity. A carriage charge will be levied for small orders.

Please do no hesitate to contact me, should you require further information.

Yours sincerely

Peter Lee
General Manager

GRANTING CREDIT
Letter 90: Notifying a buyer about a discount for prompt payment

This request adopts a formal tone but is nonetheless quite friendly. On most occasions it would be unusual to enclose a letter with a statement. If you are suggesting a special arrangement, or this is a new benefit which you are introducing for the first time, it is worth enclosing a letter drawing it to the customer's attention.

IDENDEN INDUSTRIES
A division of Idenden Plc
Porter House, Hull HU7 4RF England

Tel 01482 119087 Fax 01482 119088
Registered in England No: 1218943

Michael North
Sales Director
Beta Engineering Co
Silver Street
Foxhill
Swindon
SN3 7NM

30 May 1999

Dear Mr North

Please find enclosed our statement as at 31 July for £2903.86.

We have pleasure in offering a prompt payment discount with this invoice of £87.12. To claim it, our account must be credited with the full amount of £2816.74 within seven working days of the date of this invoice, otherwise I regret we must ask you to pay £2903.86.

We look forward to receiving your payment.

Yours sincerely

John Goodge
Finance Director

This type of letter is likely to raise a few hackles and may prove controversial with some of your better-established customers. Attempting to change general terms and conditions once trading has begun is bound to produce some resistance. When the terms affect the amount that (potentially) has to be paid, it is likely to produce some waves. You must be prepared to lose some customers who prefer to obtain their supplies elsewhere.

The advantage of this term is that those who do pay on time should not really have any reason to object, since it is not directed at them, while if they are likely to be affected you should be questioning whether to do business with them anyway.

Note the need to obtain the written agreement of your customers to introduce the term.

IDENDEN INDUSTRIES
A division of Idenden Plc
Porter House, Hull HU7 4RF England

Tel 01482 119087 Fax 01482 119088
Registered in England No: 1218943

Mr B Holmes
Marketing Manager
Beresford-Biggs Ltd
39 Cavalry Drive
Histon
Cambs
CB7 4FE

16 July 1999

Dear Mr Holmes

Credit surcharge
As I am sure you are aware, the current economic climate is pressurising supplier and customer alike. The continued high cost of credit now means that we are obliged to insist upon prompt payment of our sales invoices, within the agreed terms of 30 days net.

A 5% credit surcharge will apply to all sales invoices from 3rd August.

A value of an equal amount will be allowed as a prompt payment discount, provided that full payment is received within 30 days of date of invoice.

This will be rigorously applied, as we can no longer fund the extended credit that a small percentage of our customers is abusing.

You have placed an order for wing nuts with us; before we process this further, I am obliged to seek your written agreement to our terms of trading.

Please sign this amendment to our terms of trading and return it without delay.

Yours sincerely

John Goodge
Finance Director

I agree to the application of a credit surcharge of 5% on all my invoices and I agree that, in the event of my payment exceeding the 30 days limit, I shall not deduct the surcharge but accept it as a valid invoice item and remit the debt in full.

Signed B Holmes............................

For Beresford-Biggs Ltd   Date:

If you sell low-cost items that would take a lot of administrative time in credit control, it is probably not worth giving credit on the items unless your customers are regular buyers. Here, the product costs only £32.90. If the debtor decided to delay payment, any profit on the sale would soon be swallowed up in having to send collection letters. With the certainty of payment in advance, you can be confident that your profit remains intact.

H J KINGSLEY (NORWICH) LTD

Kingsley House, Morris Street, Norwich NR6 7JM
Tel: (01603) 117097 Fax: (01603) 117099 Reg. No: England 12086215 VAT No: 8793519

Mr G Johnson
General Manager
Taylor & Ball
25 South Lane
Norwich
NR4 5EK

16 June 1999

Dear Mr Johnson

Your order no. FG6799
Thank you for the above order.

We enclose our pro forma invoice no. SD2495 for £32.90.

When we receive your remittance, the goods will be despatched to you the same day.

Yours sincerely

Barry Fuller
General Manager

Occasionally, a customer may get into cash-flow difficulties and notch up a record of poor payment. Even though the cash-flow problems may be temporary, it is prudent to consider withdrawing the credit terms that the customer was previously permitted.

Note in this letter how the supplier makes it explicit when the goods will be despatched, not simply when the cheque has been received but when it has cleared through the account.

The final sentence should help to take some of the sting out of the mistrust that is conveyed – although the customer has only himself to blame.

⊛ **WILSON SMITH LTD**

A wholly-owned subsidiary of The Wilson Group PLC
16 Willow Walk, Retford, Nottingham NG6 8WS
Tel: (01777) 121211 Fax: (01777) 121233
Reg. No: England 1212298762

Mr Brian Adams
Production Director
FGH Products Ltd
Unit 8 Potters Lane Ind. Est.
Almondvale
Perth
PH1 2EL

29 September 1999

Dear Mr Adams,

Re your order no. TE3156
Thank you for the above order.

Your previous payment record precludes us from offering you our normal credit terms. We therefore enclose our pro forma invoice No. BN8164 for £456.76.

If you would like to send us a bank draft for the amount or arrange a credit transfer to our account, we shall gladly supply you with the items ordered by return.

Alternatively, we can accept a cheque, although the goods will not be despatched until the amount has cleared through our account.

We regret having to impose these stringent terms on you and hope that we may soon be able to resume a normal trading relationship.

Yours sincerely

Jim Tay
Finance Director

REFUSING CREDIT
Letter 94: Complaining about credit terms not being adhered to

The tone of this letter is stern, with an undercurrent of irritation. The customer is playing the old game of ignoring agreed terms and paying when he feels like it. Listing the sequence of events (showing yourself as being completely reasonable and the customer's accounts department as completely unreasonable) gives greater weight to your actions when you announce that credit is being withdrawn.

Note how the supplier defines the credit terms of "...30 days...". This is important, because some companies mean literally 30 days from the date of the invoice, while others mean (as here) at the end of the month following that in which the invoice is issued. Another effective technique is use of the rhetorical question in the penultimate paragraph "I wonder when it would have been?", which underlines your lack of trust in the customer.

Grange & Turner Ltd
32 WESTBOURN ROAD, WITNEY, OXON OX6 7HY

Telephone (01993) 107888
Fax (01993) 107843

Reg. No: England 13078453
VAT No: 75698764

Mr A Scott
General Manager
Scott Bros
Morton House
Station Road
Glasgow
G6 7HY

13 September 1999

Dear Mr Scott

I am writing to you because I want you to know of our experience when attempting to be paid on agreed terms by your company.

Names are rented by your company from our mailing lists department. Terms agreed, and signed by your company secretary, are "30 days", i.e. payment is due at the end of the month following that in which the invoice is issued.

Yet repeatedly we are told by your accounts department that the terms are 60 days. Colleagues have phoned and spoken to the people who place the orders with us and carefully reminded them of the agreed terms. And yet nothing changes.

On 17 April, I 'phoned to request payment for a February invoice. I was told "we pay on 60 days". That day I wrote to Helen Winters, who had placed the order.

Today, having had no reply, I phoned her – to be told that she has left. And when I spoke to the accounts person, I was told that "a cheque will be put in the post today".

Despite all those previous conversations, 78 days from the date of our invoice, on agreed terms of 30 days, your cheque has not even been mailed. I wonder when it would have been?

Given this experience I am sure that you will understand when I say that I can no longer make credit facilities available to your company. Any future orders will have to be paid for in advance.

Yours sincerely,

Jane Markham
Finance Director

REFUSING CREDIT
Letter 95: Writing off a debt and refusing to supply a company

This is a variation of a letter asking a customer not to come back, ever.

The phrase "...it will give us great pleasure..." sounds as if it is preceding a compliment so it is a shock for the reader when the compliment turns into a pointed insult. Its meaning is clear and uncompromising and no one receiving such a letter will be in any doubt about the intention.

RPP Holdings Plc
35/38 New Road, Paignton, Devon TQ3 4UU
Tel: 01803 175653 Fax: 01803 187908
Reg. No: England 1976143

Attn. Brian O'Neil
Taylor & Shaw Ltd
Grafton Way
Exeter
Devon
EX447MB

27 January 1999

Dear Sir

We note that you have failed to respond to our previous demands to settle the debt of £34.80 that you owe this company

Should you ever wish to receive items from this company in the future, it will give us great pleasure to refuse you.

Yours faithfully

Tom Richards
Finance Director

HANDLING QUERIES
Letter 96: Enclosing a copy of an invoice requested

If you are asked for details about an invoice, try to give as much information as possible: not only the invoice number, but also the customer's purchase order number, its date and, if possible, the name of the person who placed the order.

Thomas King & Palmer Ltd

serving the world

24 Fuller Road, Welling,
Kent DA16 7JP
Tel : (01322) 100132
Fax : (01322) 100178

Reg. No : England 1212298762
VAT No : 92905643

Frank O'Neil
Marketing Manager
Benton Copleys
Roundtree House
Kennet
Newmarket
CB8 7LP

25 June 1999

Dear Frank,

Thank you for your fax dated 20 June.

I enclose a copy of our Invoice No. 85930 as requested. These items were ordered against your Purchase Order No. 45844, dated 1 May and signed by Hazel Partridge.

I hope this clears up the matter but, if you do have any other queries, please do not hesitate to contact me.

Yours sincerely

Bill Vail
Accounts Manager

Setting your debts to a business against theirs to you, is another trick accounts departments like to play.

The difficulty with this arrangement (as highlighted here) is that, unless the trades are simultaneous and the payment terms identical, it means that one side inevitably obtains more credit than the other. No wonder someone is going to cry 'foul'.

Highlighting how many days it has taken for payments to arrive (or not to arrive) is another smart technique to use. The precision accentuates the point and creates a stronger impact than simply saying that payment is 'overdue'.

SIMPSON & MARTIN

39 TOP STREET
STOKE-ON-TRENT
ST2 3DR UNITED KINGDOM
Tel: (01782) 156232 Fax: (01782) 120899
Reg. No: England 96223978 VAT No: 91210674

FAX MESSAGE TO: Brian Johnson
                    ALF Services Limited
                    Maid House, West Road, Reading
                    Fax No: 01753 956717

From: William Patterson   Date: 1.10.99

Re Overdue Invoices

I was astonished when I telephoned your accounts department this morning to enquire when our July invoices would be paid, to be invited to accept setting them against your invoices to us not yet due. I thought that it was only fair that you were put in the picture.

I have sent the following message to Tracey Macer, who requested this:-

"Here is a copy of our order No 101687, which resulted in your invoice D4/09210 and credit D40931. You will see that terms agreed with Brian Johnson included payment '30 days from mailing date'."

The relevant mailing date was 15.09.99. Payment is not yet due.

The payment which I am requesting from ALF is for invoices dated 11.7.99. According to the terms signed by ALF (copy follows) payment was due 30 days later. Today, 82 days later, we have not been paid.

You have asked me to accept setting Simpson & Martin's debt to ALF against ALF's debt to Simpson & Martin. This I cannot accept. ALF's debt is very much overdue, whilst Simpson & Martin's is not yet due.

I reserve the right to treat agreed credit terms in the same way ALF treats them.

I would be grateful if you would arrange immediate payment of your overdue account with us.

ALF's history of payment is not brilliant. In the last year it has taken more than 100 days for us to be paid for some invoices.

Regards

William Patterson
Finance Director

HANDLING QUERIES AND DISPUTES
Letter 98: Informing a customer that a statement has already been paid

Occasionally, you may find that statements are accidentally duplicated. (It can be surprising how many companies who receive a duplicate invoice actually pay it as well!) This letter should sort matters out.

Note the way this letter closes. This is a useful phrase that can be applied in any situation where you want to signal that you don't expect to hear from the supplier's accounts department again.

IDENDEN INDUSTRIES
A division of Idenden Plc
Porter House, Hull HU7 4RF England

Tel 01482 119087 Fax 01482 119088
Registered in England No: 1218943

Jim Little
Marketing Director
York Plastics
54 East Street
York
YO9 8BM

22 February 1999

Dear Jim,

We have recently received the enclosed statement from you.

We are at a loss to know why this should have been re-issued, as the sum in question was paid directly to your bankers from our bank on 19th February 1999.   I enclose a copy of the advice from our bank.

I hope this matter can now be considered closed.

Yours sincerely

John Goodge
Finance Director

If you find yourself on the receiving end of an irate creditor on the warpath for their money, this letter should help to appease him.

Note how the 'reasons' are very conveniently side-stepped, with an all-embracing phrase (which could be used on a multitude of occasions) that explains they are "...both tedious and convoluted." A super phrase that says absolutely nothing but will leave the other side with the impression of a good story left untold.

The last sentence should help to restore the creditor's faith in you; implying the invoice "...slipped through the net..." makes it sound like a one-off mishap.

Taylor Taylor & Shaw
Benton House, Clifton, Bristol BS16 7LJ
Tel: (0117) 1089254   Fax: (0117) 1089211

FAX MESSAGE

To: Sally White

Fax No: 0181 756 9841

From: Peter Pope   Date: 23 June 1999

THIS MESSAGE CONSISTS OF ONE PAGE. PLEASE LET ME KNOW BY PHONE OR FAX IMMEDIATELY IF ANY PAGE IS ILLEGIBLE.

Dear Ms White.

Re: Your Fax of 7 June 1999
First, apologies for the delay in replying to your fax, which was caused by the absence of Michael Taylor and myself on business travel overseas.

Your invoice no. CP25648 will be settled in full on Monday, when we should have received a corresponding cheque from Ferdinand Ramos of Marco Leathers Inc., which has been couriered to us from their offices in the Philippines today.

The reasons for the delay are both tedious and convoluted. Suffice it to say, your cheque will be despatched by special delivery on Monday, with a copy sent to you by fax to confirm despatch.

Should any future invoices 'slip through the net', please do not hesitate to bring it to my personal attention and I will attempt to resolve the problem immediately.

Regards

P Pope
Financial Manager

Partners: AW Taylor & GS Taylor

RESPONDING TO REQUESTS FOR PAYMENT
Letter 100: Advising an international customer that payment is on its way

This is a pleasant, disarming letter. It sounds completely genuine. Saying you are "...extremely embarrassed..." should put the other side off their guard. Blaming your accounts department is OK (provided you won't get into their bad books). "I hope we haven't done our reputation too much harm" demonstrates your concern and how much you empathise with your supplier's plight.

 RPP Holdings Plc
35/38 New Road, Paignton, Devon TQ3 4UU
Tel: 01803 175653 Fax: 01803 187908
Reg. No: England 1976143

FAX MESSAGE TO: Mr M Wong, Financial Director

FAX No: (852) 2189 3698

FROM: T. Richards, Financial Director DATE: 4 October 1999

THIS MESSAGE CONSISTS OF ONE PAGE. PLEASE LET ME KNOW BY PHONE OR FAX IMMEDIATELY IF ANY PAGE IS ILLEGIBLE.

RE: YOUR INVOICE No 118597 DATED 7 AUGUST 1999

MESSAGE: I have today sent by international courier a cheque in the amount of £1070, in full settlement of the above invoice.

I am extremely embarrassed over the long delay – a result, I am afraid, of our accounting department not being as familiar as I am (and as they should be) with currencies other than the US Dollar.

Please accept my assurances that we will do everything to ensure that this kind of delay is not repeated in future. I hope we haven't done our reputation too much harm.

Regards

Tom Richards
Finance Director

If you think you may need to use the services of your lawyer, it is best to ask in advance what sort of bill you are likely to incur in recovering the debt. This will probably influence your decision about whether to take legal action or how far down the road to go.

The lawyers may be a bit cagey on costs, because a lot will depend on the time needed. If they sound unwilling to give you a indication, ask what their hourly charging rate is. Having an idea in advance, and warning a lawyer of impending action, will save you time if you need to instruct them quickly.

H J KINGSLEY (NORWICH) LTD
Kingsley House, Morris Street, Norwich NR6 7JM
Tel: (01603) 117097 Fax: (01603) 117099 Reg. No: England 12086215 VAT No: 8793519

Mr J H Jones
Jones, Turner & Hills Partners
34 Frost Avenue
Norwich
NR3 7TF

23 June 1999

Dear Mr Jones,

Re: JW Mann (Packagers) Ltd
We have an outstanding debt of £12,501.90 with JW Mann (Packagers) Ltd. We have sent them a final demand for payment but I have heard on the grapevine that they are experiencing some severe cash-flow difficulties and I am not hopeful that we shall receive payment within seven days.

If we do not receive payment in that time, I would like to instruct your firm to issue proceedings against JW Mann. Before we do, though, I would appreciate an estimate of the foreseeable costs (including your disbursements) that we are likely to incur, assuming our claim is undisputed.

If you are unable to give us an estimate, please give us details of the hourly charging rate of your firm and, from your experience, a rough approximation of the number of hours that a case of this nature might take.

I am confident that our case is very strong and that no credible defence will be made to our claim.

Yours sincerely

Tim Good
Finance Director

Appendix 1
301 ways to start your letter

As discussed ... requested ... agreed ...

As discussed, will you please send ...
As discussed, I enclose samples of ...
As discussed, I am very sorry for the delay in sending you ...
As requested, I enclose ...
As we agreed this morning, I would like to confirm our mutual decision ...
At our last meeting, it was agreed that ...

As you are aware ...

As I am sure you are aware, ...
As I have previously explained to you, ...
As you are aware, under our holiday policy, the company reserves the right ...
As you are no doubt aware, there are certain confidential and personal files ...
As you are no doubt aware, the recent events in ...
As you know, we deal with a number of different suppliers ...
As you know, we have been working ...

Congratulations ...

Congratulations.
Congratulations on winning ...
Firstly, Mary, I would like to say how delighted I am for you at your news ...
Many congratulations on the birth of your son.
May I be the first to offer you our congratulations on ...
I was delighted to hear you have won ...
I would like to offer you my personal congratulations ...

I am sorry ...

Firstly, apologies for the delay in replying to your fax, which was caused by ...
First of all, my sincere apologies for not responding to your enquiries ...
Firstly, I would like to say how sorry we are that you have had to wait so long ...
I am sorry if this messes you around but our client has just notified us that ...
I am sorry that you feel that you have not received the level of service expected.
I am sorry that you feel the price of ...

I am sorry to hear that you are unable to trace ...
I am sorry to learn of your recent bereavement.
I am very sorry that you were left waiting ...
I am very sorry to hear that you are still not making a good enough recovery ...
I am very sorry.
What can I say? Sorry.
Oops! We've made a real clanger.
We were all very saddened to learn about the sudden death of your wife ...
We were deeply shocked by John's untimely death ...
We were shocked and saddened to hear of Howard Green's fatal accident.
I was very sorry to hear your sad news.
I write as one of Howard's new customers to say how very, very sad we were ...

Following ...

Following our conversation this morning, I am delighted to confirm our offer ...
Following our telephone conversation ...
Following the recent accident involving ...
Following the staff meeting this morning, I am writing to confirm that ...
Following your claim for ...

Further to ...

Further to our recent discussion, I have pleasure in enclosing ...
Further to our recent telephone conversation, I have pleasure in enclosing ...
Further to our telephone conversation, I am writing to introduce you to our ...
Further to your fax this morning: at the moment I am feeling very let down by your ...
Further to your recent conversation with ...
Further to your request for ...

I ...

I note from my diary that you have an appointment to see me on ...
I promised to let you have details of ...
I realise that I should not have ...
I recently saw details of your company's range of ...
I telephoned your office last week for a revised quotation ...
I think it was very useful to talk through your performance over the last six months ...
I don't dispute that other customers have accepted ...
I wrote to you on the 16th September chasing the above order for ...

I am surprised ... disappointed ...

Bob, you personally gave me your word and I trusted you to pay promptly ...
I am surprised to have had no response to my fax dated ...
I am surprised to have received no reply to our previous letter ...
I am afraid that our Financial Director has put these orders on hold ...
I am at a loss to understand why you have not paid us the monies which you owe.
I am extremely disappointed that I find myself having to write to you yet again.
I am now getting very concerned that we have heard nothing from you ...
I am very disappointed that you have not remitted the sum of ...
I am very disappointed with you.
I hoped that I would not have to write to you about ...
I have now sent you a number of fax messages and am disappointed ...
We regret to note that you have failed to respond to our previous reminders ...

I am pleased ...

I am pleased to confirm your appointment as agent for ...
I am pleased to inform you that the company agrees to ...
I am pleased to quote you ex-works prices for the items, as requested.
I am delighted to confirm that you are this year's winner of ...
I am delighted to report that we have had an excellent year ...
I am delighted to say that our sales are ahead of expectations ...
It was a pleasure to meet you and Richard in February ...
It was a pleasure to meet you yesterday, ...
It was great to meet you and your team last week.

I have received ...

I have received a consignment of ...
I have received in the post this morning your invoice no. ...
I have received your catalogue of ...
I am in receipt of your fax of 10 February.
I am in receipt of your letter of 30 June, asking for a reference for ...
I received a copy of your autumn catalogue, giving details of ...
I received, this morning, your invoice no. ...
Yesterday, we received ...
We received your delivery of ...
We today received from you ...
We have received an application from ...

I am writing ...

I am writing concerning your request for a refund ...
I am writing on a matter that is causing ...
I am writing to advise you of a change in our terms and conditions ...
I am writing to clarify the position about the ...
I am writing to confirm our telephone conversation, regarding ...
I am writing to express my growing dissatisfaction of the service we are receiving ...
I am writing to let you know that we have decided not to renew your contract ...
I am writing to thank you for recommending me to ...
I am writing to you because I want you to know of our experience ...
I am responding to the idea that you put forward ...

I confirm ...

I confirm our faxed quotation for ...
I confirm our quote of ...
I confirm that, as of today, we are amending your terms of contract ...
I confirm the points we discussed at our meeting on ...
Just a note to confirm our conversation today ...
Just a quick note to confirm the deal agreed ...
I would just like to confirm that we have considered your request to ...
I write to confirm our order for ...
Confirming my telephone call and your return fax, ...
This is to confirm our meeting at your offices at 10.30am tomorrow, 25 January.
This is to confirm the details and the key terms of the offer we have accepted ...

I enclose ...

I enclose, herewith, a draft copy of ...
I enclose our purchase order for ...
Please find enclosed our cheque to the value of ...
Please find enclosed our statement as at 31 July for £2903.86.

It is ...

It is not often I receive such an abusive letter. In spite of your rude tone ...
It is with a tinge of sadness that I have to announce ...
It is with regret that I tender my resignation as ...
It has come to my attention that you ...
It was useful to review your progress to date ...

I have ...

I have been advised by ...
I have been given your name by ...
I have checked my records and realise that ...
I have considered your letter of 21st January and your assertion that ...
I have just been reviewing ...
I have just come across a product that is so good ...
I have just received your ...
I have just returned from a visit to ...
I have now reviewed your proposal to ...

I hope ...

I hope the last order we supplied to you was satisfactory and met your expectations.
I hope you and Joshua are well and that you are not having too many sleepless nights.

I refer to ...

I refer to our order dated ...
I refer to our order for ...
I refer to our telephone conversation this morning.
I refer to your letter of 11 February.
I refer to your letter of 23rd April 1999 about a consignment of ...

I trust ...

I trust that you enjoyed your break.
I trust that you received our consignment ...
I trust that you have received my previous correspondence.

I understand ...

I understand from my colleague, ...
I understand from our Mr Davies that you are considering moving ...
I understand that, to obtain the price that is right for us, you have asked us to take ...
I understand that you are concerned about the amount of time you have been given ...
We understand that ...

I was appalled ... astonished ... concerned ...

I was appalled to learn that our consignment had not arrived on time with you.
I was astonished when I telephoned your accounts department this morning ...
I was extremely concerned to hear that you have not received ...

I was most disturbed to receive your letter of 20 April, informing me of ...
I was very disturbed to receive your letter, concerning ...
I was given your verbal assurances on Tuesday that you would have no problem ...

I would like to ...

I would like to correct a factual error in your ...
I would like to place a firm order for ...
I would like to remind you of our agreement ...
I would like to tackle a problem that we have come across, ...

Many thanks for ...

Many thanks for agreeing to act as our ...
Many thanks for the cheque for £...., received this morning.
Many thanks for the letters received from both John and yourself, concerning ...
Many thanks for your enquiry for ...
Many thanks for your excellent talk, which ...
Many thanks for your latest offerings.
Many thanks for your letter, asking if we are prepared to offer ...
Many thanks for your letter of 13th January.
Many thanks for your order, received today.

Please ...

Please arrange for the consignment of ...
Please let me have a price on Tuesday 4 April for ...
Please find enclosed our cheque to the value of ...
Please find enclosed our statement as at 31 July for £2903.86.
Please find attached our order for ...
Please find our cheque to the value of £1123.60 to cover our order ...
Please supply a quotation for the following: ....
Please supply and deliver as follows: ...

Thanks for ...

Thanks for coming in to see me last week.
Thanks for coming to put the ...
Thanks for looking into the possibility of arranging ...
Thanks for sending through the latest price changes.
Thanks for your delivery of ...
Thanks for your quotation for ...
Thanks for your fax of 9th May. Sorry that I have sat on it for so long ...

Thank you ....

I felt I had to write to you to say how delighted I have been with ...

Just a note to say thank you for the cheque.

Just a quick note to thank you very much for your time the other day ...

Thank you for allowing me time to assess the above product.

Thank you for applying for a Credit Account with us.

Thank you for asking if we would be interested in buying ...

Thank you for attending the interview last week for the post of ...

Thank you for being so frank and open about the difficulties that you have ...

Thank you for bringing the lower than expected performance to my attention.

Thank you for buying ...

Thank you for coming to see me last ...

Thank you for contacting me about ...

Thank you for letting me know about ...

Thank you for returning the ...

Thank you for sending ... ...

Thank you for taking the trouble to clarify the situation for me.

Thank you for the business which you have brought to us.

Thank you for the courtesy extended to me during my visit to ...

Thank you for your application for a credit account.

Thank you very much indeed for your extremely pleasant letter ...

Thank you very much for arranging a most enjoyable day for me.

Thank you for your ...

Thank you for your application for the post of ...

Thank you for your cheque for £1500 in part settlement of your account.

Thank you for your comments on our proposed discount.

Thank you for your completed application form for the position of ...

Thank you for your enquiry about the price of ...

Thank you for your fax, which I received this morning, asking if ...

Thank you for your fax, regarding payment for your orders.

Thank you for your invoice no. ...

Thank you for your kind invitation to ...

Thank you for your latest delivery, received today

Thank you for your letter dated 17th February, addressed to our Managing Director, which has been brought to my attention.

Thank you for your letter dated 9th September, addressed to our Managing Director, who has passed this to me for my attention.

Thank you for your letter expressing concern about the service you are receiving ...

Thank you for your letter of 11th September and for the samples ...

Thank you for your letter of 12 June, concerning the carriage charge on our invoice.

Thank you for your letter of 12 June, outlining the terms ...

Thank you for your letter of 15 July, notifying us that ...

Thank you for your letter of 20 June, regarding ...

Thank you for your letter of 21 May, advising us ...

Thank you for your letter of 24 June, applying for the post of ...

Thank you for your letter of 26 January, asking about the terms for ...

Thank you for your letter of 3 June, enquiring if we have any vacancies for ...

Thank you for your letter of 30 April in response to our order ...

Thank you for your letter of 3rd December and for your kind comments.

Thank you for your letter of 7th March, which reached me today.

Thank you for your letter of the 5th July, expressing concern over ...

Thank you for your letter, querying the price of ...

Thank you for your order against our quotation no. ...

Thank you for your payment of £..., which, I note, was credited to our account ...

Thank you for your prices, received this morning.

Thank you for your proposed price ...

Thank you for your recent enquiry.

Thank you for your recent faxes. I apologise for the delay in replying.

Thank you for your recent order for the enclosed ...

Thank you for your recent order. I am afraid that we have temporarily sold out of ...

Thank you for your recent telephone call, regarding ...

Thank you for your request for a reference for ...

Thank you for your suggestion that we ...

Thank you for your telephone call today.

Thank you for your time on Tuesday, concerning ...

Thank you very much for your letter about ...

We...

We are a small company, specialising in ...

We are currently seeking to be registered ...

We are in receipt of your cheque for ...

We are intending to trade with ...

We are interested in ...

We are pleased to announce the appointment of ...

We are reorganising the administration of our accounts department ...

We have an outstanding debt of ...

We have been notified by ...

We have considered your request to operate an agency ...

We have decided to change the holiday policy of the company.

We have just learned about the death of ...

We have just secured an unexpectedly large order ...

We have noticed some abuses of the telephone for private calls ...
We have recently received the enclosed Statement from you.
We have reviewed the price changes to our products for the next 12 months.
We have supplied you with items on four separate occasions to the value of ...
We met at the Multimedia 99 show (on the Wednesday) and you showed me ...
We no longer need ...
We note that you have failed to respond to our previous demands to settle ...
We wish to obtain ...
We would like to carry out some amendments to ...

With reference to ...

With reference to our recent telephone conversation, ...
With reference to our telephone conversation, I have pleasure in introducing ...
With reference to the above, we have received ...
With regard to the above, we enclose ...
Re: your fax to our accounts manager of ...
Re: your recommendation of ...

You ...

You have been issued with ...
You have been specially selected to receive one of our star prizes ...
You have received two written warnings about ...
You may have heard rumours circulating ...
You supplied us with a new ...

Your ...

Your account has been passed to me for attention ...
Your account with us is now SERIOUSLY OVERDUE.
Your company has opened a credit account with us.
Your customer ... has applied to us for a credit account ...
Your subscription to ... will be expiring within the next three months.

More notes to start on ...

A week ago, you arranged for ...
According to my records, you still owe ...
As a company committed to providing a quality service, ...
As you are a valued customer, we want every pound you spend with us to save you money.
Having arrived back safely ...

Here is our ...
In April this year, you ordered ...
In case you failed to receive the details we sent last month of our fabulous ...
In conversation with your colleague, Mary, yesterday, it emerged that ...
In response to your telephone enquiry this morning, I am writing to announce that ...
Just a quick note to let you know that ...
On 30 September, we placed an order for ...
On 6 August, we received from you a consignment of ...
On a recent visit to your company, I left our company brochure for your attention ...
Our agreement of 20 January stipulates that you undertake to supply us with ...
Payment for this order was due in ...
The response to our advertisement for an Office Manager has exceeded ...
Since we have acquired ...
Something very peculiar appears to have been happening with ...
Until now, it has been a requirement of the company that everyone ...
With the departure of ...

Appendix 2

201 nice turns of phrase

This appendix selects over 200 of the best phrases for you to choose from. It concentrates on phrases with mood and emotion so, whether you are having to write a letter of condolence, persuade someone to your way of thinking or bring a supplier up sharply, you are certain to find the right phrase to fit the moment.

Stern phrases

I trust our purchase order instructions will be rigidly adhered to in future.

As they have not been received by the due date, we are exercising our right under the agreement to cancel the order forthwith.

I was surprised to see a carriage charge included for ...

No mention was made of this charge ...

Our purchase order referred expressly to the fact that delivery was to be included in the price ...

You may recall that when I placed the order, you granted us a special discount ...

... it should be little more than an extension of what your current practices are ...

We expect our suppliers to give us the service that we demand ...

It will certainly make us think twice about using you in the future ...

Unless you can agree to do our printing profitably within the price agreed, we will probably have to agree to part company.

I expect a full refund by return.

We shall have no option but to seek an alternative supplier.

I am therefore bound to advise you that ...

Please give it your most urgent attention.

It is time this matter was brought to a close.

... we shall not hesitate in disallowing the commission payment ...

... it is naturally disconcerting ...

It is also particularly disappointing ...

You have not had the authority ...

I was led to believe that this was included in your quotation

... your failure to notify us ...

Your conduct in this matter has been extremely disappointing ...

I was very disturbed ...

... we have already had to make several representations ...

We object in the strongest terms ...

I hope this makes our position clear ...

We expect you to accomplish it within the agreed deadline and budget.

We must have a solution if you are to retain our custom.

I regard this behaviour as totally unprofessional.

I am not satisfied that the goods are of merchantable quality.

Since the goods are not fit for the purpose intended ...

I must stress that, in placing this order with you, ...

... it was absolutely conditional on your ability to meet our deadline.

... for which we shall seek compensation.

I was astounded to find that ...

... we shall be seeking recompense for any losses that we incur.

... the occasion was a shambolic disaster from start to finish.

I strongly sense that you are taking us for granted ...

... the entire job is simply unacceptable...

I am particularly irritated that, once again, you are blaming ...

I am hoping that you will take these issues more seriously than your colleagues
appear to ...

Contractual phrases

Under the terms of our agreement ...

... I trust that you will abide by the terms of our agreement.

I would like to draw your attention to the agreement...

Our agreement expressly forbids you ...

... in full and final settlement ...

... it was a condition of our contract ...

As you have not kept to the terms of your contract ...

... failure to comply with our terms ...

... we shall have no option but to terminate ...

... we are exercising our right not to pay ...

... we undertake to rectify ...

... we have made good the defect ...

... we have honoured our contract to you ...

... we shall have no option but to terminate ...

Letting someone down lightly

At the moment, it does not fit in comfortably with our plans for the immediate future ...

I am afraid I must say "Thanks, but no thanks".

Our decision was arrived at after a great deal of discussion and thought.

It was not an easy decision to make ...

While I believe that your experience is right for us, ...

I am confident that you would be able to secure a good number of orders for our business but ...

... it would not be fair to either of us ...

Phrases that trigger people's emotional responses

You will understand that, as a business, we put a high premium on reliability.

I am feeling very let down by your company ...

... don't have a moral leg to stand upon ...

... really should know better ...

It was not we who caused this problem ...

Phrases that charm customers

... as a special favour ...

... enclosed is the guarantee which sets out our promises and your rights ...

We look forward to a long and happy association with your business.

Should we fall short of your high expectations in any matter ...

... please contact me personally.

... and trust that this helps in compensating you for your dissatisfaction.

We are, of course, concerned to offer you the best possible service ...

... as you are a highly valued customer ...

Anticipating that this arrangement will be acceptable to you, I have pleasure in enclosing ...

... you have been specially chosen ...

... we are asking a select group of our customers ...

... you will avoid immeasurable hassle ...

Making a gentle request

... we will have to ask you ...

... I do not consider it unreasonable to ask you to ...

I don't want to put you to any trouble, but it would be enormously helpful ...

I appreciate this is a busy time for you, but I wonder if ...

It therefore does not seem unreasonable to request ...

Phrases that aim to reassure

I confirm that we are happy to stand by our original quotation.

I assure you it is perfectly normal and will not impede its function.

... it does not fulfil the high standard that we demand and you, as a customer, expect.

... would not dream of stepping beyond the powers ...

I am appalled at how you have been treated ...

I was most disturbed to receive your letter ...

... the intention is not to squeeze a quart out of a pint pot.

... before you come running to us crying 'foul' ...

I know how frustrating it is to be left high and dry ...

I trust everything is in order ...

Making sincere apologies

If I could perhaps explain the circumstances that occurred, not as an excuse, but so you can see the exceptional and unexpected difficulties that we faced.

I am deeply sorry that we have let you and your client down ...

This unfortunate event has highlighted a gap in our procedures.

I am extremely sorry this has occurred ...

This is a very rare occurrence (it happens about once a year) ...

Please accept our unreserved apologies.

I have made enquiries and have discovered that in this instance one of our internal procedural systems failed.

I do hope that this will go some way to restoring your faith in us.

It seems you have been plagued by gremlins on this occasion.

I have pushed you to the front of the waiting list ...

We are all real people in this company, who try very hard indeed to give a fast and efficient service.

I am sorry that you feel that you have not received the level of service expected.

I am confident that you should not experience the same level of disruption now.

I am sorry for any inconvenience caused.

I apologise for this oversight ...

Refusing and rejecting

I regret that we are unable to assist you further in this matter.

For this reason, I regret we must decline your kind invitation ...

I am sorry that we cannot be more helpful on this occasion.

Although, as is clear, I do not agree with much of your letter ...

... I very much regret that we must insist ...

While we do not like to impose unnecessary restrictions ...

I regret that we have decided not to take your application further on this occasion.

I have to be completely honest and say that there is no way we can pay ...

... I wish to deny in the strongest terms possible ...

... we refute your claim.

... I cannot think of any circumstance in which I would dream of agreeing ...

I do not accept your assertions ...

Persuasive phrases

... the charge reflects a contribution only towards the final cost ...

... we do everything we can to keep the charges as competitive as possible ...

... all our suppliers accept it, without exception ...

... we shall have no option but to seek an alternative supplier.

... I guarantee that you will experience the best ...

... we have striven to keep the price increases to an absolute minimum ...

... we see this as a modest contribution towards our continued mutual success ...

... it would not be in our best interests ...

... we are taking on the chin the cost of inflation and the increased cost of ...

Chasing payment

We have now decided to take legal advice on this matter, with a view to the recovery of our money ...

... instructions will be issued to our solicitors to proceed against you.

... please arrange immediate settlement.

... this thorny issue of payment ...

... remit this by return ...

... in view of the one-sided nature of our correspondence ...

... the matter will be passed into other hands in seven days.

... I hope you will render this action unnecessary ...

If you have sent your remittance in the last few days, please disregard this letter.

No further reminders will be issued.

We appreciate this act of good faith ...

... despite our best efforts to obtain payment from you ...

Responding to requests for payment

The reasons for the delay are both tedious and convoluted.

Should any future invoices slip through the net ...

I am extremely embarrassed about the long delay ...

Praise, flattery and recognition

... because you are the best person for the job ...

I will respect your decision, whatever it is.

... thank you personally for all the hard work ...

Thank you once again for your major contribution ...

... the best minds are devoted to this project ...

... I am delighted to announce that you are eligible to receive ...

Congratulations on taking the initiative ...

... I am very impressed by their versatility ...

Your role in this is, of course, pivotal.

... I applaud your enthusiasm for not missing a sale ...

It will be a tremendous honour ...

It gives me great personal pleasure to recognise ...

Threatening to take legal action

While we have no quarrel with your business ...

... we intend to take legal action against ...

... unless she agrees to abide by the terms of our agreement ...

... we shall commence legal proceedings against her.

Warnings

I must warn you ...

... we find it inexcusable ...

... failure to do so ...

You have been given every opportunity ...

As you have chosen to ignore all the warnings ...

... we have no alternative ...

... you must not undertake ...

... you were unable to give us a satisfactory reason ...

Offering help and assistance

... we shall be only too happy to provide ...

We will do everything we can to help ...

... I shall be keeping my fingers crossed.

Motivational

... I know you will be very capable of successfully accomplishing ...

You have a great deal to contribute ...

I am confident that there will be considerable opportunities to increase your responsibilities.

I know you will do your utmost ...

I know you will be able to make a major contribution ...

... it is a tribute to your hard work ...

It means a great deal to me, personally, ...

Condolence

We were deeply shocked ...
... it will be very difficult for us to forget ...
We will miss him sorely.
Please accept our sincere sympathy.
We were shocked and saddened ...

Selling phrases

... will cut a swathe through the tasks ...
By far the best, ever.
... that makes the guide, for me, utterly irresistible.
... quickly and confidently ...
Do have a look at it ...
... a return that is <u>absolutely guaranteed</u>.
... you do not, absolutely not, have to buy anything from us ...
What do you have to lose?
I have just come across ...
... we felt it essential to let you know about it ...
Just complete the fax-back acceptance offer ... before everyone else does.
... outstanding value for money ...

Appealing for donations

... go a little way to help ...
... find the heart to help ...
... It's not a lot to ask ...

Keeping your options open

Your payment terms are subject to the timing of our payment runs.
However, we reserve the right to return ...

Keeping a supplier firmly on the hook

I accept this as a gesture of apology but not as a satisfactory recompense for the late
   delivery.

Exaggerating a point slightly

It has cost us up to £400 more a month ...

Preparing the ground for bad news

I very much regret that, as from 1st May, we must increase prices of this product ...

Appendix 3
185 ways to finish your letter

Best ...

Best regards.
Best wishes.
Best wishes and good luck.
Best wishes from myself and all at ...

I ...

I am grateful that you took the trouble to write ...
I am returning the item with this letter and expect a full refund of ...
I am sorry for any inconvenience caused.
I am sorry that we cannot be more helpful on this occasion.
I do hope that this will go some way to restoring your faith in us.
I enclose a stamped addressed envelope for your convenience when you reply.
I have pleasure in enclosing ...
I have pleasure in returning the product as required ...
I must insist that, from now on, we are given priority treatment.
I regret that we are unable to assist you further in this matter.
I therefore look forward to your immediate reassurance ...
I very much regret that we shall be unable to offer you a refund.

I hope ...

I hope that we continue to be of benefit to you in the future.
I hope they are a success for you.
I hope this arrangement is acceptable to you.
I hope this arrangement is satisfactory.
I hope this explains the position but, if you have any other queries, please do ask.
I hope this information helps you.
I hope this makes our position clear.
I hope this matter can now be closed.
I hope this plan meets with your approval.
I hope this proposal will be of interest to you.
I hope you are willing to help us in this matter.
I hope you have a very successful and prosperous New Year.
I hope you will be able to agree to this proposal.

I look forward to ...

I look forward to a long, fruitful and communicative business relationship.

I look forward to a long and prosperous association with your company.

I look forward to continuing a close relationship with your business in the future.

I look forward to hearing from you and, of course, to receiving your order.

I look forward to hearing from you at your earliest convenience.

I look forward to hearing from you shortly.

I look forward to hearing from you, with regard to ...

I look forward to hearing from you.

I look forward to meeting you all again soon.

I look forward to meeting you.

I look forward to receiving confirmation of your order.

I look forward to receiving your remittances by return.

I look forward to receiving your reply.

I look forward to seeing you again shortly.

I look forward to seeing you on your next visit to the UK.

I look forward to your advice on this matter.

I look forward to your further enquiries.

I look forward to your immediate response.

I trust ...

I trust that further action will now be taken and look forward to your response.

I trust that you find these of interest.

I trust that you will abide by the terms of our agreement.

I trust this gives you the information that you require.

I trust this is a satisfactory summary of our conversation.

I trust this is all in order and hope that you are satisfied with the goods as supplied.

I trust this summarises our conversation satisfactorily.

I trust you will take the above into account.

I would ...

I would appreciate it if you could amend your records accordingly.

I would appreciate it if you could settle the account by the end of this month.

I would be grateful if one of your representatives could telephone me ...

I would be grateful if you could arrange for ....

I would be grateful if you could confirm safe receipt.

I would like to take this opportunity to wish you every success in your future.

If ...

If anyone has any queries about this new policy, please come and see me at any time.

If I can be of any further assistance to you, please do not hesitate to contact me.

If not, please arrange immediate settlement.
If there is anything we can do, please let us know.
If this is of interest, let me know.

If you ...

If you are interested in any of these, do give me a call.
If you are still unable to locate the item, please let me know.
If you do not receive the items by next Tuesday, please let me know.
If you have any further queries on this matter, please contact me again.
If you have any further questions, please do not hesitate to contact me.
If you have any more queries, please do not hesitate to contact me.
If you have any queries, please give me a call.
If you have any queries, please contact me on ...
If you have any questions, or need any further information, please give me a call.
If you have sent your remittance in the last few days, please disregard this letter.
If you need further information, please do not hesitate to contact us.
If you require any further information, please do not hesitate to ask.
If you would like further information, please ring us on ...

In the meantime ...

In the meantime, please could you arrange for ...
In the meantime, I shall ensure that ...
In the meantime, if you have any queries, please give me a ring.

It ...

It is essential that these instructions are adhered to, strictly.
It is time this matter was brought to a close.
It would be appreciated if you could let me know, by return.

Kind ...

Kind regards
Kindest regards.

Let me know ...

Let me know if this is of interest to you.
Let me know if you find out any details and, once again, many thanks for your help.
Let me know what you decide. I will respect your decision, whichever way it goes.
Let me know your thoughts.

Many thanks for ...

Many thanks for your co-operation.
Many thanks for your help.
Many thanks for your prompt and courteous attention to this matter.
Many thanks for your time and effort on our behalf.

Once again, ...

Once again, please accept our sincerest apologies.
Once again, please accept our apologies.
Once again, my sincere apologies.
Once again, thank you very much indeed for taking the trouble to write to me.

Please accept ...

Please accept my apologies for this delay.
Please accept our most sincere condolences and deepest sympathy, from all at ...
Please accept our sincere apologies for the distress caused.
Please accept our sincere apologies for this slight deterioration in service.
Please accept our sincere sympathy for your loss.
Please accept our unreserved apologies.

Please ...

Please advise me of ...
Please call me back urgently, so we can discuss this.
Please cancel ...
Please come back to me if it does not solve the problem.
Please confirm whether this time is convenient for you.
Please arrange for the balance to be supplied as soon as possible.
Please give this matter your most urgent attention.
Please let me know if anything goes wrong again.
Please do not hesitate to call me, should there be any issue that you want to discuss.
Please do not hesitate to contact us, should you need any further information.
Please do not hesitate to get in contact, if we can be of further assistance.
Please find enclosed a copy of our current price list, as requested.
Please give me a call if you would like to set up a meeting.
Please give me a ring if anything is unclear.
Please let me know if this arrangement is of interest.
Please let me know if you think this outline plan is suitable.
Please let me know when these samples will be sent.
Please, please, please supply us with the missing items ASAP.
Please telephone me on receipt of this letter, to let me know ...

Please transfer the remaining balance to account no. ...
Please try to answer these queries quickly, to enable us to ...

Should you ...

Should you be uncertain about any aspect of it, please do not hesitate to give us a call.
Should you have any urgent enquiries, please do not hesitate to contact me personally.
Should you require any further information, please do not hesitate to contact us.

Sorry ...

Sorry for any inconvenience caused by this matter.
Sorry for any trouble caused.

Thank you ...

Thank you again for your assistance, and all good wishes for a successful ...
Thank you for the interest you have shown in our Company.
Thank you for your assistance in this matter.
Thank you for your attention to this matter.
Thank you for your co-operation with this policy.
Thank you for your co-operation in this matter.
Thank you for your help with this matter.
Thank you for your interest in our range of products.
Thank you for your interest.
Thank you for your kind attention.
Thank you for your time and efforts on our behalf.
Thank you in advance for your co-operation.
Thank you, once again, for your kindness.
Thank you once again.
Thank you very much indeed for taking the trouble to write to reassure me.
Thanking you in advance.
Thanking you in anticipation of your assistance in this matter.

We hope ...

We hope never to hear from you again.
We hope you find the package of value and look forward to your future custom.

We look forward ...

We look forward to a long and happy association with your business.
We look forward to hearing from you.
We look forward to helping you save money throughout the coming year.
We look forward to receiving your payment.

We look forward to seeing you then.
We look forward to welcoming you as a customer.
We look forward to your valued, continued support.
We look forward to receiving your cheque by return.

We ...

We regret, therefore, that we must decline your kind offer.
We shall keep you informed, as and when developments occur.
We thank you for this order and look forward to your further enquiries.
We very much appreciate your help in this matter.
We would appreciate your quotation by fax and at the latest by Thursday 12 June.

With ...

With kind regards.
With very best wishes,

Would you ...

Would you kindly acknowledge receipt of this letter and confirm ...
Would you kindly arrange for someone to come and ...
Would you please confirm that ...

Your ...

Your immediate response (and payment) would be appreciated.
Your order will be dispatched as soon as we receive your remittance.

More notes to end on ...

A quick reply would be much appreciated.
Any future orders will have to be paid for in advance.
As stated, we will be having no further dealings with your company.
Do let me know what you decide and I shall be keeping my fingers crossed.
Finally, I enclose the form duly completed and signed.
Give me a call to let me know when you are coming.
Hope to speak to you soon.
Just tick the box on the enclosed reply-paid envelope and send it back to us.
May we take this opportunity of thanking you for your valued support during ...
Regards.
The agenda for this meeting is attached.
This does not help to foster confidence in our business together.
To find out how we can help you, call me now on ...
Whatever the cause of the delay may be, we must have a solution ...

Index

T

U

V

W